EXTREME TRAUMA

October 7
as an Outlier in the Range of Human Potential

EXTREME TRAUMA

October 7
as an Outlier in the Range of Human Potential

The Event
The Resiliency
The Future Hope

Compiled by Moshe Kaplan M.D.

An educational project of the *Be A Mensch* Foundation

Extreme Trauma: October 7 as an Outlier in the Range of Human Potential
Compiled by Moshe Kaplan, M.D.

Copyright © 2024 American Friends of Be A Mensch Foundation, Inc. All articles and essays in this book are Copyright © 2024 by their individual authors.

All Rights Reserved.

This book, or any portion of it, may not be reproduced or transmitted electronically, mechanically, or by any other means including but not limited to photocopying, scanning, downloading, etc., without prior written permission of the author. For sales inquiries, contact: info@beamensch.com.

Copy editing by Ruth Leah Kahan
Typesetting by the Virtual Paintbrush
Cover design by Hodaya Cohen

ISBN 979-8-218-48287-9

First edition August 2024

Published by the Be A Mensch Foundation
www.beamensch.com

Dedication

This book is dedicated to those who value truth and are committed to upholding and living with it.

"Truth is the cry of all but the game of few."
– George Berkeley

Special Tribute

To Joe Lieberman,
Chairman of the *Be A Mensch* Foundation
and a real *mensch*

Joe was an exemplary public servant,
an American patriot, and a matchless champion of the Jewish people and the Jewish State

He was a man of integrity, decency,
and civic courage.

He had deep moral sense as well as common sense, and was fearless in his defense of truth.

He was also extraordinarily kind
and a loyal friend.

There are few people who would be heralded by all as an exemplary *mensch*.
Joe Lieberman was one of them.

The *Be A Mensch* Foundation was privileged to have him as our Honorary Chairman.

He was a credit to the Jewish community and will be missed by all who knew him.

Congratulations on compiling this book.
I hope it influences many.

Joel S. Sandberg M.D.
Eye Surgery Associates
www.browardeyedoctors.com

State of Israel
Ministry of Foreign Affairs

מדינת ישראל
משרד החוץ

17.2.2025

To whom it may concern,

The book "Extreme Trauma" telling the story of the 7th of October is a very important and unique book.

The book contains both the story of the trauma giving a wide picture of the events but unlike many other books it is going further to share the story of the amazing civic resilience that was so powerful and so inspiring.

The book also includes a clear view of a better future, it is portraying a path to a future with real hope for Israel to grow and prosper.

The author Moshe Kaplan MD created a book which is both a special guide to the events and to the greatness of so many who made it possible for Israel to
fight and survive.

I highly recommend the dive into this book that will no doubt serve as a tool in telling our story as it is done in the book with a lot of love and grace.

Dan Oryan
Director of the Civic Diplomacy
MFA

דן אוריין
מנהל מחלקת דיפלומטיה

Att: Moshe Kaplan MD
An educational project of the Be a Mensch Foundation

משרד התפוצות והמאבק באנטישמיות
לשכת המנהל הכללי

בס"ד

27 פברואר 2025
כ"ט שבט תשפ"ה

Subject: Book recommendation

I have read and reviewed the book "Extreme trauma".

I believe the book is important for delivering the truth about the trauma of October 7th but also noteworthy is delivering a message of hope and Jewish resilience.

Anyone who wants the complete story as well as what they can benefit from this tragedy will find this book useful and an excellent read.

Ron Brummer

Deputy Director General

Ministry of Diaspora Affairs and Combating Antisemitism

Acknowledgments

WE, AT THE *Be A Mensch* Foundation (beamensch.com) are grateful to all of the wonderful people who volunteered their time to offer input to this educational project.

Special thanks to Yoram HaCohen, Adv. and his staff; to Hannah Hartman, who typed, organized, and improved the manuscript; our editor, Ruth Leah Kahan, who assisted in tightening, correcting, and clarifying the text, while diligently preserving the authors' original voices; Felice Eisner, who did the final work of structural organization, copy editing, and cohesion; and to Shanie Cooper at the Virtual Paintbrush, whose skillful layout made the book's presentation aesthetic and clear.

Table of Contents

Foreword
Moshe Kaplan, MD, Wendy Singer 1

Introduction
Moshe Kaplan, MD 3

    Bunkers of Death (Kan News Editor Recordings)

CHAPTER ONE: HUMAN POTENTIAL: UNLEASHING GREATNESS 11

What Is Greatness?
Abraham J. Twerski, MD 13

Acts of Human Kindness
Moshe Kaplan, MD 16

This Man Rescued 120 People on Oct. 7th
by Sarah Pachter, Aish.com 19

CHAPTER TWO: ANTISEMITISM AND ISRAEL 27

The BIG Lie
Moshe Kaplan, MD 29

    The Nazi Era: The Origins of the Big Lie

    Post-War Antisemitism and the Foundation of Israel

> The Role of Ivy League Universities
> The Impact of Boycotts and Cultural Boycotts
> Media and Social Media: Amplifying the Lies
> The Role of NGOs and Activists
> Confronting the Big Lies

The Delusional Version of Events: Unmasking the October 7th Propaganda
Moshe Kaplan, MD..35

> Denial of the Mass Rape Perpetrated by the Hamas Barbarians
> Manipulation of Casualty Figures
> The UN's Role in Propagating Misinformation
> The Myth of the Mass Grave at Nassar Hospital
> The Happy Hostages Hoax
> Amnesty International's Misguided Reports

The BIG Truths: Israel's Sense of Moral Responsibility
Moshe Kaplan, MD.. 39

> Israel's Efforts to Counteract Hamas's Propaganda

CHAPTER THREE: THE SILENT CRY — HAMASTICIDE (APOCALYPTIC BARBARISM) 43

Civilization versus Barbarism: An Irreconcilable Clash?
Moshe Kaplan, MD...45

Setting Things Straight — Hamas Are Not "Militants," They're Terrorists!
Nils A. Haug 48

> Contrasting Ideologies: The Stark Differences between the IDF and Hamas
>
> Gazan Perspectives: The Complex Views on Hamas and the October 7th Attack
>
> A Double Standard: The World's Hypocritical Stance on Israel

Inside Hamas: How the Terrorist Organization Uses Guerrilla Tactics to Wage War
Darcie Grunblatt for the Jerusalem Post, July 13, 2024 59

> Using residential buildings, civilian homes for stockpiling weaponry
> Ambushing Israeli soldiers

Hamasticide: Apocalyptic Barbarians at the Gates of Israel
Fiamma Nierenstein.. 66

> The Descent into Barbarism in the World

The Silent Suffering: Revealing Hamas's Brutality and Global Silence
Moshe Kaplan, MD, based on articles written by Yvette Alt Miller on Aish.com..86

Why the World Loves Hamas and Hates Israel
Noa Tishby 95

No Peace with Terror: International Community Must Support a Hamas-Free Future
Ari H. Orkaby 99

The Most Evil Society in Human History
Gary Willig..103

Charles Manson and the Bibas Victims of Hamas
Rabbi Yair Hoffman 108

The New 9/11
Gary Willig.. 114

CHAPTER FOUR: PSYCHOPATHOLOGY OF SEXUAL ABUSE 119

The Women's Movement Has a Double Standard When Sexual Violence Happens to Jews
Meredith Jacobs.. 121

The True Face of Israel's Enemies: The Roots of Psychopathological Sexual Abuse
Moshe Kaplan, MD 127

> *Hamas's Strategy for Creating a False Perception of Reality*
> *The Art of Deception*
> *The Psychological Underpinnings Behind Hamas's Strategy*
> *The Palestinian Authority: Complicity in Terrorism*
> *International Enablers: UNRWA and Beyond*
> *The Reality of Radicalization*

The Horrors of Genocidal Rape: Understanding the Psychopathology Behind It
Moshe Kaplan, MD 133

Multiple Perpetrator Rape: A Deeper Look into the Origins of Hamas's Behavior
Moshe Kaplan, MD 136

The World Looks Away
Moshe Kaplan, MD 138

> *Women's Groups Defending Hamas*

Silent Cry: Sexual Crimes in the October 7 War
Karmit Klar-Chalamish, PhD 142

> *Abstract*
> *Opening Remarks*
>> *Orit Sulitzeanu, Executive Director — The Association of Rape Crisis Centers in Israel*
>
> *Introduction*
> *About the Association of Rape Crisis Centers in Israel*
> *Background: Sexual Crimes in War*
>> *Characteristics*
>
> *Implications*
>> *Psychological Implications*

    Physical Implications

  Methodology

    On the Process of Collecting Evidence: "But why aren't they speaking?"

  Findings

    First Analytical Axis: Arenas

    The "Nova" Festival

    Kibbutzim and Villages in the South

    Israel Defense Force (IDF) Bases

    In Captivity

    Second Analytical Axis: Mapping Patterns of Sexual Assault

  The Practice of Rape During War

    Systematic Use of Brutal Violence to Commit Rape

    Multiple Abusers/Gang Rape

    Rape in the Presence of Family/Community Members

    Sexual Offenses of Males

    Execution During or After the Rape

  Sadistic Practices

    Binding and Tying

    Mutilation and Destruction of Genital Organs

    Insertion of Weapons in Intimate Areas

    Destruction and Mutilation of the Body

  Summary

  Endnotes

Male October 7 Survivor Recounts Rape at Hands of Hamas Terrorists
Times of Israel Staff (24/07/2024) 179

Unmasking the Horrors: Hamas's Weaponization of Sexual Violence — Summarizing the Facts
Moshe Kaplan, MD 183

CHAPTER FIVE: RESILIENCE..................................... 189

Everything Is a Miracle
Moshe Kaplan, MD.. 191

Unyielding Resilience — The Jewish Spirit from Ancient Trials to Modern Heroism
Moshe Kaplan, MD..192

National Resilience — The Key to Winning the War
Miriam Adelson, MD..195

    What Is Resilience?

    A National Trauma

Israel's Indomitable Spirit: Emerging Stronger from Adversity
Moshe Kaplan, MD..198

Building Resilience and Standing Against Hate: WIZO and Hadassah's New Initiatives
Carol Ann Schwartz... 201

Rising from Ruins: The Journey of the Israel Trauma Coalition
Israeltraumacoalition.org 204

A Beacon of Hope: The Journey of Attorney Hanan Alsanah
Moshe Kaplan, MD..207

Leading the Way Forward: Ben Gurion University's Remarkable Resilience
Sourced from The Hartman Institute event, May 8, 2024......... 211

    Alon Jacobs — wounded BGU Industrial Engineering and Management student-reservist

    Talia Meital Schwartz Tayri, PhD — AI for SW lab at BGU

    Galit Katarivas Levy, PhD — Department of Biomedical Engineering

Rising from Ashes: The Inspirational Journey of Israel's

Amputee Soccer Team
Moshe Kaplan, MD..212

Resilience Amid Adversity: Israel's High-Tech Sector Stands Strong
Moshe Kaplan, MD..216

The 48 — 2024
Israel 21c..219

A Story of Unity and Hope: Surviving Hamas Captivity
Amelie Botbol, Jewish News Syndicate, May 14, 2024 234

The Heroic Escape of Yarin Shriki: A Tale of Survival and Strength
Amelie Botbol, Jewish News Syndicate, May 29, 2024 237

Stunning Speech by Menahem Kalmanson, October 7th Hero, Upon Receiving the Israel Prize for Civic Heroism
Yehuda Dov, VINnews, May 15, 2024 240

We Are a Miracle
Yaakov Shwekey 243

What It Means to Choose Life
Douglas Murray..246

CHAPTER SIX: UNITY — THE SAVING GRACE 255

Unity
Moshe Kaplan, MD..257

A Message of Hope: Reclaiming Our Stories
Moshe Kaplan, MD..259

Israeli Comedian Announces That He Will Keep the Sabbath for the First Time
Vered Weiss, World Israel News 262

Unity in Adversity: President Herzog's Call to Action
Moshe Kaplan, MD 264

A Fissiparous People
Moshe Kaplan, MD 266

> *The Power of Unity: Lessons from the* **Be A Mensch** *Foundation Acheinu Worldwide Achdut Program*

New Exhibit at Hostage Square Aims to Inspire
Unity and Healing
Israel National News, March 31, 2024 271

Stronger Together — One Nation, One Heart
Moshe Kaplan, MD 274

APPENDICES **275**

APPENDIX A: About the Authors

- Miriam Adelson, MD 277
- Yvette Alt Miller, Phd 278
- Cochav Elkayam-Levy, PhD 278
- Brig. Gen. (ret.) Meir Elran, PhD 280
- Nils A. Haug 281
- Rabbi Yair Hoffman 281
- Meredith Jacobs 281
- Moshe Kaplan, MD 282
- Karmit Klar-Chalamish, PhD 283
- Douglas Murray 283
- Fiamma Nirenstein 284
- Ami H. Orkaby 284
- Sheryl Sandberg 286

Carol Ann Schwartz 286

Yaakov Shwekey 287

Wendy Singer 287

Noa Tohar Tishby 287

Abraham J. Twerski, MD 288

Gary Willig 289

APPENDIX B: The **Be A Mensch** Foundation 290

APPENDIX C: Sources 293

Foreword

BUT FOR THOSE who do not subscribe to Hamasticide (apocalyptic barbarism) there is another option — using one's human potential to fulfill the ideals of the Be A Mensch Foundation: consideration, tolerance, respect, and love.

The Be A Mensch Foundation was founded on these ideals and seeks to instill them in Israeli society.

The contributors to this book have made truth the pervasive value, and have engaged in creative efforts to bring the salient facts of the tragedy of October 7th to the public's awareness, and to educate the global community.

Through this book, the Be A Mensch Foundation is reaching out to those who recognize human potential, share the vision for a united nation, and appreciate the opportunity to participate in making the world a better place. It exposes the evil that occurred on that day, and contrasts it with the values of an ethical and moral life, while offering us all the hope for a better future, with its examples of the many aspects of Israeli resilience.

MOSHE KAPLAN, MD

TERRORISTS GETTING READY to tear through the Gaza border fence into Israel. Their screams of joy and maniacal energy were bone-chilling. Is this how the Nazis sounded?

It was hard to fathom that human beings could wake up and decide, "This is what we are going to do today."

On the other hand, telling about what happened on October 7th is one of the most important acts that journalists and other documentarians who live during this period can undertake.

Wendy Singer (Israel 21c)

Introduction

EXTREME TRAUMA IS a collection of unique essays and opinion pieces inspired by the events of October 7. They highlight not only what took place on that dark day, but also focus our attention on the resilience of the Israeli populace and the future hope emerging from new found unity and purpose. There are no words in the English language to describe the despicable, depraved, barbaric actions of Hamas on October 7th and since that day. It was "Hamasticide" (apocalyptic barbarism).

However, those individuals who recognize the opportunity that life offers will use their existential potential to improve themselves and make the world a better place in which to live.

Theories about the psychopathological behavior of Hamas abound. These terrorists and their allies justified the use of sexual violence and abuse for their deranged activities. We have sourced some of these.

The Rape Center in Tel Aviv, Israel, has documented much of the barbarians' activity. The Jewish people has a long history of being physically and spiritually abused. Nevertheless, we are a resilient people. We have flourished and will continue to do as long as we are unified.

The events of October 7th brought unprecedented unity to the Israeli people and most of American Jewry.

This is our saving grace. In some cases, especially with regard to the hostages, events transpired after those selections had been published.

Moshe Kaplan, MD

Bunkers of Death (Kan News Editor Recordings)

THE HORRIFIC MASSACRE of Supernova music festival attendees who came under attack in the roadside "bunker of death" outside of Kibbutz Re'im was captured in a three-hour phone recording, excerpts of which have been released in recent days.

Ayelet Arnin, 22, a news editor with Kan News who was murdered inside the shelter, instinctively started a recording of the experience as terrorists began their onslaught on the morning of October 7. The recording documents less than half of the seven-hour ordeal inside the shelter, ending a few hours before survivors were rescued.

In that recording and others, released in a one-hour episode of Kan's documentary series *"Zman Emet,"* those who hid in the roadside shelter can be heard trying to defend themselves against the Hamas-led terrorists who had come to murder and kidnap them, while trying to comfort one another as the massacre of the festival-goers unfolded.

In the episode, video clips initially showed the group of frightened revelers arriving at the bomb shelter, videoing the initial barrage of rockets. As more people arrived at the shelter, they began to receive more information on the dangerous developing situation.

"They began to fire at us now," Laor Abramov, 20, who was eventually murdered in the shelter, is heard telling the group in a video, adding that he and his friends were shot at nearby.

The group is then heard coming to the realization that they are unable to flee due to the ongoing attack outside.

Speaking to Kan, Ziv Abud, who survived the massacre, recalled that Aner Shapira, who fended off the terrorists before being killed, told them that there was a "huge terrorist invasion, this is not normal."

At 7:52 a.m., at the start of Arnin's recording, terrorists are heard yelling in Arabic outside the shelter.

Segev Israel Kizhner, 22, Arnin's good friend who was later murdered, is heard noting, "They saw our cars."

"I can't believe they're already here, please G-d," Arnin says.

"Put your phone on silent," Kizhner urges.

Terrorists are then heard outside trying to enter the shelter. At this point, Kizhner tries to calm Arnin, who expresses fear over the sounds of Arabic outside.

"I can't listen to this Arabic," Arnin says.

"You have to be quiet," Kizhner responds.

Hearing explosions in the background, those inside wonder whether security forces are finally arriving. (They would take much longer to do so, far too late for most of those inside the shelter.)

Osama Abu Assa, 36, a Bedouin security guard at the party, is heard in the recordings leaving the shelter to speak to the terrorists.

"Raise your hands! Raise your hands!" a terrorist is heard saying.

"I am a Muslim," Abu Assa responds, pleading with them to stop, as a terrorist continues to yell at him to raise his hands. Those in the shelter are heard crying during the confrontation.

"Come out, come out," a terrorist is heard yelling, and commands Abu Assa to lie on the ground, guns aimed at him.

"Are there Jews inside?" a terrorist asks him.

Survivors cited by *The New York Times* said that Abu Assa "pleaded with the gunmen not to enter the building" and murder those hiding inside.

At 7:56 a.m., Kizhner is heard calling out that a terrorist had thrown a grenade into the shelter, urging someone to throw it back. Lidor Levi, 28, is then seen on dash cam footage trying to bolt out of the shelter, before being shot dead by the terrorists. At the same time, Shapira throws the grenade back out of the shelter.

Nitzan Rahoum, Levi's fiancee, who was pregnant, is heard in the recordings calling out her partner's name. "They took Lidor," she is heard saying. She was later killed.

"He is outside," Itamar Shapira, a survivor of the massacre (no relation to Aner), is recorded responding.

"They're throwing grenades at us. I don't know what's happening here. I can't believe we're sitting ducks here," Kizhner is heard saying, while also trying to comfort Arnin.

Another grenade is thrown in, then thrown back out by Shapira, followed by an explosion and crying, as heard in the recordings. Eight grenades in total were thrown and tossed out by Aner Shapira.

At 8:01 a.m., someone is heard saying: "Don't move, don't move, get down."

"Guys, step away from the wall," a terrorist is heard telling others. A grenade is again thrown in, then hurled back outside by Shapira.

Kizhner tells Shapira, "You're a fighter, brother," as others encourage him to continue his brave defense.

Itamar Shapira tells him, "Throw all those grenades." Arnin says: "What a king."

At 8:02 a.m., Itamar Shapira asks those around him, "Are we trying to call the police?" Someone responds that they are calling, but police aren't answering.

When another manages to reach the emergency police line, he is heard saying: "Hi, you have to come to Kibbutz Re'im. Quickly, before something serious happens. There are terrorists outside at the bus stop. We're stuck in the shelter. They're throwing grenades at us here. Twenty people, outside there are dozens of armed men."

Kizhner urges those present, "Put your head down, put your head down, everyone put your heads down. You have to, now."

At 8:05 a.m., Abud also gets into contact with the police, when suddenly, a grenade explosion is heard on the edge of the shelter.

People are heard trying to calm one another. Then Alon Ohel, speaking to the police, is heard saying, "Come as quickly as possible, please, please."

Kizhner is heard telling Ohel to relay to police that security forces should bomb the armed men from above.

"[The policeman] told me, 'Try to hide, bye.' What does that even mean?" Kizhner says.

Arnin responds: "That they are doing what they're doing, I don't know."

At 8:06 a.m., another grenade is thrown out, and an air force jet is heard above, with Kizhner heard expressing hope they would bomb those outside.

Aner Shapira is then heard saying, "No, no," which is followed by the sound of an explosion, possibly the grenade that finally exploded in his hands, killing him.

"Baby, are you ok?" Itamar Shapira is heard asking his

girlfriend, Agam Yosefzon. Crying is heard in the background. Ohel is heard calling police again, pleading with them to come, as another grenade is thrown in.

"No, no, no, they're shooting at us endlessly, we're all bleeding here," he tells the police.

"You have to get away," a policewoman is heard telling him.

"It's impossible, it's impossible, we're in the shelter. It's impossible," Ohel responds.

"Someone is dead," a person is overheard saying. "What happened now?" the policewoman asks.

"They're firing at us, someone has died," Ohel says, apparently referring to Aner Shapira.

By 8:09 a.m., Ohel is recorded continuing to beg police to rescue them, as Kizhner laments there is no one left to protect them.

"Alon, if there is another grenade, you have to throw it out. We need someone to throw the grenades out," Kizhner says.

Another grenade is thrown in, and Tamar Samet, 20, says in a panic, "I threw it there, there, there!" She was later murdered.

Kizhner urges the group to be alert and pay attention to the bunker entrance. Another grenade is then heard being thrown in, then thrown out of the shelter. Terrorists then fire several shots at the shelter.

At 8:10 a.m., Kizhner is heard urging that another grenade be thrown out, but it explodes inside the shelter.

Hersh Goldberg-Polin, 23, is heard saying, "I don't have a hand," as someone urges that a tourniquet be tied around the wound, and Kizhner continues to say the grenades must be tossed out.

As the situation worsens, those inside the shelter begin

comforting each other and saying their goodbyes. Rahoum calls out to her friends Antonio Macías Montaño, 28, and Yvonne Rubio Vargas, 26, who express their love for one another. Both died.

Kizhner alerts Arnin that he is injured: "Are you with me, my love? I love you."

"Me too, me too," she responds.

At 8:27 a.m., the terrorists are heard taking several people hostage, as resistance to their attack dies down.

One of the terrorists says: "*Yalla, yalla*, pull him out, pull them!"

"There they are, there they are, those dogs," another says.

"Pull him out, pull him, pull by the hair," a terrorist says.

Itay Banjo is overheard saying: "Please, please."

"Come, or I will shoot you, come," a terrorist says.

"We have a family, please," Banjo is heard begging. "Help me," he adds, as terrorists urge people to come out of the bunker.

Banjo was killed by the terrorists.

"Do you work in the army?" the terrorist asks someone. Itamar Shapira is heard saying in Arabic, "Salaam, salaam," meaning peace.

Four people were taken hostage alive from the shelter: Goldberg-Polin, Alon Ohel, Eliya Cohen, and Or Levy.

After the abductions, the terrorists are heard returning to spray bullets inside the shelter to ensure others are killed. In total, 16 were murdered, while seven managed to survive and were later rescued.

Survivors are then heard spending the next two hours comforting each other and waiting.

At 8:31 a.m., Shapira is heard urging Yosefzon to hold down her leg wound. "Hold it strong, breathe, and we will live," he says. The terrorist's vehicle is then heard driving away.

At 9:47 a.m., gunfire is heard again outside.

He then asks Ziv Abud for water, but she can't reach anything due to her wound. "I'm sorry, I love you, I'm sorry," she says.

The group continues to wonder if the terrorists are still outside, and contemplate trying to leave.

Abud then calls the police again, telling them their location. At 10:59 a.m. Arnin's battery runs out and the recording ends.

In total, 364 people were murdered when heavily armed Hamas-led terrorists attacked the Supernova music festival on October 7. Some 1,200 people, mostly civilians, were killed in scenes of horror throughout southern Israel, and 251 were taken hostage to Gaza, sparking the ongoing war against Hamas.

Chapter One

Human Potential: Unleashing Greatness

"Great things are done by a series of small things brought together." — Vincent Van Gogh

"Perfection is not attainable, but if we chase perfection we can catch excellence."
— Vince Lombardi

What Is Greatness?

Abraham J. Twerski, MD

It is a blend of qualities including honesty, integrity, passion, resilience, fortitude, self-belief, and strong values. Think of all the gifts you have been given to better yourself and the world. We humans are endowed with opportunity and potential. To actualize our potential, we must combine our good desires and intentions with our understanding. How we use the skills we are blessed with will determine whether we make the world a better place or bring it down.

Man can ascend, charged with spirit and energy to do good and benefit creation, or he can merely exist without a higher purpose. Growth is change, and although positive and desirable, it is change nonetheless. Our natural tendency is to avoid discomfort by maintaining the status quo. However, rather than viewing discomfort as an impediment to growth, we should recognize it as a signal that it is time to advance to a new stage of development. The practical implementation of this understanding is the key to greatness. We all need to account for how we use our most valuable asset — time — and whether we are honest in our affairs. Pursuing true values, such as self-improvement and making the world a better place, will lead us to greatness.

We can help others become better and achieve their potential. Johann Wolfgang von Goethe said, "Treat the other person as he is and he will remain as he is. But treat him as he ought to be and could be, and he will become what he ought to be and could be."

A human being enters the world in an essentially animal state, seeking only the gratification of his desires. If a person remains driven solely by desires, restrained only by the desire to avoid pain, he has not advanced beyond the animal stage. He might be intelligent, but he is merely an intelligent animal, or as science designates, a *homo sapiens* — an intellectual baboon. Intelligence alone does not elevate a person above this level.

Homo sapiens can achieve contentment, but true human excellence surpasses mere contentment. True human potential and happiness are realized when we rise above base desires and strive for goals beyond self-gratification. Failure to do so leads to frustration and depression, often resulting in indulgence or the pursuit of artificial euphoria through substances. Ironically, we achieve true happiness when we seek the perfection of being a *mensch* — often through the denial of physical urges rather than their gratification.

A human being becomes truly humanized when he implements potentials unique to mankind. These include:

1. Learning from the history of past generations.
2. Searching for truth.
3. Reflecting on the purpose and goals of life.
4. Self-awareness.
5. Volitionally improving oneself.
6. Contemplating the future and considering the consequences of actions.

7. Being considerate of others and sensitive to their needs.
8. Sacrificing comfort and possessions for the welfare of others.
9. Empathy.
10. Making moral and ethical choices despite strong bodily drives.
11. Forgiveness.
12. Aspiring.
13. Delaying gratification.

These uniquely human features constitute the human spirit, and spirituality is the actualization of these potentials. According to this definition, non-spiritual man is merely an intelligent animal. Many psychological and physical illnesses afflicting humans stem from indulgence or escapism. Indulgence extends beyond sex, food, and drugs to include ego-driven behaviors as well. Developing character, which is spirituality (as defined above), can eliminate many human afflictions that result from being on an unproductive, stagnant treadmill of exertion without growth.

Holism has become a popular concept, referring to considering a person as a physical unit rather than as an assemblage of parts. However, true holism involves developing spirituality, completing the being that G-d intended, and achieving the happiness of being truly a human being — a *mensch*.

Acts of Human Kindness

Moshe Kaplan, MD

The October 7th attack on Israel brought in its wake thousands of stories of "ordinary" people rising to the occasion and providing every kind of support, comfort, care, and resource imaginable for those in need. Here is just one example:

The Fandel Family

During the barbarous attack on October 7th, in the courtyard of a quiet house in Moshav Shuva, the Fandel family ran a private rescue operation. Dr. Gedalya Fandel set up and managed an improvised emergency room and field hospital at the junction leading to the moshav, treating numerous wounded with limited resources, while facing a medical and psychological crisis of unprecedented proportions. All day long he cared for a nonstop influx of shell-shocked soldiers and injured civilians. He also dealt with a pile-up of bodies that were dropped off at his makeshift hospital for "safekeeping" until they could be dealt with properly.

Meanwhile, his wife Merav and their children managed the home command, offering survivors of the massacre a safe haven with a kind word, a listening ear, games of

Rummy, warm food, and beds — ensuring safety, emotional support, and comfort for everyone who came to find refuge. The welcome and hospitality they gave the survivors offered a calming semblance of normalcy amid the chaos. Their home became a brief shelter for many, including two children who had witnessed their parents' murder, and a pregnant woman seeking safety.

As the day wore on, neighbors and other residents of the moshav joined in their efforts, offering additional help and resources.

The Fandel family's actions exemplify human kindness and the power of community support during times of unimaginable crisis.

Human potential is a boundless force waiting to be unleashed. As we've seen through these acts of kindness and bravery, our greatest achievements come from our capacity to care for, support, and uplift one another. Each of us has the potential to make a significant impact on the world. By embracing our unique human qualities and striving for greatness, we can create a better future for ourselves and for generations to come.

The journey to greatness is not a solitary path but a collective endeavor. It is through our shared humanity and communal efforts that we rise above challenges. However, it is within the power of each of us as individuals to be the *mensches* who will inspire change. Our actions, no matter how small, contribute exponentially to a greater good. G-d and the universe are waiting for each of us to actualize the greatness within us, making the world a better place for all. This is the foundation for "normative" human behavior.

Having expressed the particulars of human potential, we are going to describe what happens when a person, instead of using his gifts for good, uses them to produce tragedy, disaster, and inhumane behavior. In Chapter Two we will explore the dynamic of this deviant behavior.

This Man Rescued 120 People on Oct. 7th

by Sarah Pachter
Aish.com

On October 7th, farmer Oz Davidian risked his life, driving back and forth to the Nova Festival site and surrounding areas fifteen times to save youngsters and bring them to safety. "I knew that there were people dying and no one was there to help them. I kept going back. I knew that I had been placed there by G-d. I could not ignore what I was seeing. My only regret is that I was not able to save more."

On the morning of October 7th, Oz and his family were awakened by the sound of rockets overhead. "Living in the south, we've learned to recognize various kinds of missiles and this was obviously an unusual attack." Oz lives only five minutes away from the site of the Nova Festival and the sky was laced with flashes of light as the rockets were being intercepted.

After receiving a WhatsApp message from a family member pleading for anyone to help the wounded, Oz was determined to help. He secured his own wife and four daughters in the safe room, locked the door to the house, and told them, "I'm going. I'll be back."

He drove out of his home in Moshav Maslul, near Ofakim, and within moments he saw people running. He asked them what was happening. The youngsters, out of breath, almost choked on their words, "We were at a party when terrorists started shooting. Many people have already been killed."

Oz brought them to safety on his family's farm. Oz grew up there and knew the roads like the back of his hand. He knew every pothole in the ground, gap in the fence, and unpaved road. "I live very close to the location of the festival, so I was familiar with the side roads, which helped me in this mission."

Feeling the responsibility to save these kids resting on his shoulders, he started driving back and forth on the unpaved roads. This saved his life because the terrorists were waiting on the main roads ready to fire at any oncoming cars.

Oz saw the sky filled with smoke and fire. He still didn't fully understand what had happened but saw dead bodies everywhere.

He found more kids fleeing for their lives and started packing his pickup truck to the brim. He saved one group of panic-stricken people, then another and another, methodically, bringing them back to safety on the farm.

"Can You Come Get Me?"

Those saved shared Oz's contact information with their friends, and people started sending Oz their location in droves, begging for his help.

One pleaded, "Can you come get me?"

Yet another wrote, "Please help us. There are many of us here. At least five."

Others wrote that their friends were wounded in the stomach or had even died.

Oz asked for their location and went directly to that spot. This was how he saved 120 young people.

"I was very scared. I have a wife and four kids. But I also knew that there were many kids in there and they had no one to help them."

Oz's List

When he dropped them off, he had them write their names on a piece of paper. This later became *Oz's List*, the title of the documentary about his story. Oz's list grew and grew. That day he saved over 120 people's lives.

Oz shut off all emotion and shifted into autopilot. He later reflected on the miraculous nature of the day. He realized it was incredulous that he was able to enter fifteen times and survive the ordeal.

"It was very frightening each time I entered the war zone. The terrorists tried many times to shoot at me directly and they were not successful, so it is clear that there was a cloud of Divine protection surrounding me on this mission. I realized that if I would not continue, many of these children would not have made it to the other side. I am not religious in practice but I believe in G-d. I prayed that I would be successful and that I would return safely and rescue as many people as I could possibly rescue."

Some of the Nova participants asked him if he was part of the IDF. He said, "No, I am just a simple Jew who came to help."

He continued, "The children were certain that I was part of the Mossad because it was unfathomable to them that a simple guy would do such an act."

Each time Oz exited the site and drove them toward safety, he told them, "Don't look left or right. I don't want you to have to see the remnants of the day."

He tried to calm them down and handed them cigarettes to help them relax. One of the kids in the car was completely speechless and did not say a word. He was just silently crying.

Elderly Father

At one point Oz saw an elderly man, the father of a boy named Magen Par.

Magen had called his father to say goodbye. "Tell mom I love her. Do not come here, it's full of terrorists." His father ignored the warning and drove straight toward the party.

When Oz saw the old man driving his red car, he asked him, "Hey, what are you doing here? It's too dangerous for you to be here."

He answered, "If I lose my son I don't have anything. I only have one son. He's my only child and I'm not leaving without him."

Oz begged him to stay put and offered to search for his son. Shortly after Oz returned with a truck full of children. As they approached, before Oz could even stop the car, the boy jumped out of the car and embraced his father in a tight hug. Everyone was crying when they saw this reunion.

Narrow Escape

There were hundreds of bodies riddled with bullets and burnt cars scattered everywhere. Oz could smell and taste the smoke. "You see the extent of evil. You do not even see this type of horror in the movies. There was no one to protect these Jewish children."

At one point he found himself in the middle of a street that was previously rampaged by the terrorists. He saw a bike on the left-hand side and an Israeli police car right next to it. He looked closer and saw someone kneeling next to a body next to the car. "I thought it was a Jewish medic helping our own. 'Oh wow, there are medics dealing with the people, that's good.'

"I pulled up right next to him and asked, 'Hey, what's going on here? Are there more wounded that need help?'

When the man answered in Arabic, Oz realized that this was no Jewish medic. He was a terrorist who then started shooting at him point blank.

Oz pressed hard on the gas. Other terrorists started chasing him and shooting at him on all sides.

"I even saw them pulling up on motorcycles right next to me and shooting."

He managed to escape by going off road.

While escaping, Oz kept thinking about the fact that just weeks ago he was with his kids at a professional soccer game. "I kept thinking about the game and being with my family, singing and dancing. I envisioned spending happy carefree time with my children, and that gave me strength to continue. That's what uplifted me and helped me escape."

Booby Trap

Hamas even booby trapped the dead bodies. Oz searched the fields looking for signs of life. He saw dead bodies scattered everywhere. One body had a hand grenade in his hand.

Oz continued working to rescue festival goers the entire day until nightfall.

"I kept it up like a machine. I had nothing in view except bringing them out. In the middle of the day I went home for ten minutes to reassure my wife, to tell her everything is okay, to gain a little strength, and she told me, 'Go ahead. You're doing important work.'"

Oz's New Extended Family

Oz feels that each person he saved is now his child, eternally bonded.

"I consider all of the children that I brought out of the battlefield my own children. I check on them frequently to make sure they are doing well. We have created a WhatsApp group and I am in touch with each and every one of them. We meet often and speak all the time. I visit them. Many are in therapy and are recovering."

On October 30th, Oz received a Certificate of Honor from the State of Israel. Many of the survivors plan to attend the ceremony [which took place on October 30, 2024].

One couple that Oz saved plans to marry. "They expressed to me that with the help of G-d, and when they have a child, they want to name him Oz and honor me as the *sandak* at the *Brit Milah* (circumcision)."

One of the Nova participants said of Oz, "He's our angel. He came and saved us. If it wouldn't be for him, we wouldn't be here today."

Those He Could Not Save

Although there are so many who owe their lives to Oz, he was not able to save everyone who sought his help. He considers this a failure.

"There are mothers who sent me to go get their kids and I got to their locations and their kids were dead. That sits very heavy with me."

One mother sent Oz her son's location. He went to the location and saw body after body. At first he thought he was in the wrong spot.

"I kept seeing dead bodies. I did not know what to tell her. I wanted to lie to her. I told her there are many battalions of the army and that they won't let me in. It took me three and half months to build the courage to tell her the truth: that all I saw was death."

Oz's family reminds him, "The fact that there were casualties doesn't take away from everything you did. Everyone owes you a debt of gratitude."

Trauma

Healing from his trauma has been very difficult. Oz explained he had never seen so many scattered bodies riddled with bullets. "Listen, it's hard. I am still living this nightmare."

Oz has two different recurring dreams. In the first, Oz is in the field saving others. He has left the house but the terrorists are in his home, threatening his family.

In another dream, he is driving down the middle of the highway with the terrorists surrounding him. This time, though, the engine will not accelerate and he is stuck. The car will not move and he wakes up shaking in fright.

"I started going to therapy for this, but I have other dreams that creep up, too. I have come to terms with the fact that I have post-traumatic stress that will probably be with me for the rest of my life. I have to learn to live with it."

Oz attends therapy sessions with the kids he saved. "We are family for life. If I do not feel good or if I'm having a bad day, I simply call them or speak to them in the WhatsApp group that we created. They lift me up. These are my kids. They will carry me for the rest of my life.

"I want the world to understand that these terrorists did not discriminate; they killed Jews, Muslims, Bedouins, Druzim, Christians…. The impact of this attack has ripple effects across the entire world, not just for the Jewish people. We are the *Am HaNetzech*, the Eternal Nation, and we are not afraid and we are not backing down. We will not stop until we get back each and every one of the hostages. The Jewish People live and die for each other and this is our strength that no one can take away from us."

Chapter Two

Antisemitism and Israel

"Jews cannot fight antisemitism alone. The victim cannot cure the crime. The hated cannot cure the hate. It would be the greatest mistake for Jews to believe that they can fight it alone. The only people who can successfully combat antisemitism are those active in the cultures that harbour it."
–Rabbi Lord Jonathan Sacks, zt"l

The BIG Lie

Moshe Kaplan, MD

THE HISTORY OF antisemitic propaganda and manipulated truths about Jews and Israel is a long and dark one.

The Nazi Era: The Origins of the Big Lie

Adolf Hitler famously articulated the concept of the "Big Lie" in his book, *Mein Kampf*. Hitler accused the Jews of using colossal untruths to discredit Germany during World War I. He asserted that the broad masses of a nation are more easily corrupted by large-scale falsehoods because they themselves often tell small lies but would be ashamed to resort to large ones. Nazi propaganda chief Joseph Goebbels later utilized this concept, arguing that if a lie is repeated enough, people will eventually come to believe it.

The Nazis used this tactic to devastating effect, spreading lies about the Jews to justify their systemic persecution and genocide. They claimed that Jews were inherently deceitful, responsible for Germany's economic woes, and a threat to Aryan purity. They propagated these lies through state-controlled media, education, and public discourse, creating a pervasive atmosphere of antisemitism that facilitated the Holocaust.

Post-War Antisemitism and the Foundation of Israel

After World War II, the establishment of Israel in 1948 marked a new chapter in the history of antisemitism. The nascent state faced immediate hostility from its Arab neighbors, leading to a series of conflicts that were often accompanied by anti-Israel propaganda. The Arab-Israeli conflict provided a fertile ground for new big lies and manipulated truths, portraying Israel as a colonialist and illegitimate state.

In the decades following Israel's creation, various actors, including radical leftist groups and Islamist organizations, perpetuated these narratives. The Soviet Union, for example, played a significant role in spreading anti-Zionist propaganda during the Cold War, equating Zionism with racism and imperialism. Many left-wing intellectuals and activists, particularly in Western academia, adopted this rhetoric and continue to use it to influence discourse on the Israeli-Palestinian conflict.

The Role of Ivy League Universities

The influence of radical ideologies is particularly evident in Ivy League universities. Historically, these institutions have harbored fascist and Marxist ideologies, and today they witness a new form of radicalism in the form of Islamism. Journalist Daniel Greenfield points out that the support for Hamas at institutions like Columbia and Yale reflects a continuation of this trend.

Columbia University has a history of excluding Jewish students while celebrating fascist leaders like Mussolini. This admiration for fascism was common among university presidents and leaders of society during the early

20th century. Today, Columbia is a hotbed of anti-Israel sentiment, with faculty members defending students who support Hamas and other anti-Israel groups. That over 100 professors signed a letter defending students who supported Hamas's actions on October 7th underscores the extent of this problem. These professors argued that the students' actions were a response to Israel's occupation of Palestine, ignoring the brutal nature of the Hamas attack and the terror inflicted on Israeli civilians, as well as the geopolitical history of the area. Such positions reveal a deep-seated bias and a willingness to manipulate truths to fit a particular ideological narrative.

The Impact of Boycotts and Cultural Boycotts

The global movement to boycott Israeli academics and institutions exemplifies the manipulation of truths about Israel. Since the early 2000s, Western academics have made a concerted effort to isolate Israeli scholars and delegitimize Israel. This includes dis-invitations, rejections of academic work, and demands that Israeli researchers either disavow their government or face ostracism. Such actions are reminiscent of the Nazi boycott of Jewish academics and cultural figures, highlighting the continuity of these big lies across different eras.

Haaretz documented this in an article on April 12, 2023, describing an "unprecedented global boycott of Israeli academics." According to a survey that the Israel Young Academy conducted, one-third of the 1,000 senior faculty members polled reported a significant slump in their ties with counterparts abroad.

Media and Social Media: Amplifying the Lies

We cannot overstate the role of modern media and social media platforms in spreading antisemitic propaganda. Biased reports, misleading narratives, and the amplification of falsehoods on platforms like Twitter, Facebook, and Wikipedia contribute to a toxic environment in which lies about Jews and Israel flourish. Activists and organizations with anti-Israel agendas exploit these platforms to disseminate their views, often with little to no fact-checking.

The October 7th, 2023, massacre has brought to light the ongoing manipulation of truths about Jews and Israel among the masses. In the aftermath of the attack, numerous falsehoods and biased narratives emerged, further fueling antisemitic sentiments. These include accusations that Israel has engaged in genocide, colonialism, and apartheid, and they often ignore the complex realities of the conflict and the actions of Hamas.

Media bias is a significant factor of these manipulated truths. The decline of foreign correspondents and the rise of biased local stringers, often leads to skewed news coverage from conflict zones like Gaza. To amplify their effect, stringers affiliated with Hamas have been known to supply photos and reports to major news outlets, framing the narrative to suit their agenda. These news outlets rarely check the accuracy or sources of these stories. This biased reporting has had a profound impact on global perceptions of the conflict, leading to widespread misinformation and anti-Israel sentiment.

In some cases, media companies have taken deliberate steps to restrict their coverage. Matti Friedman, who worked for the Associated Press during the 2008-2009 fighting between Hamas and Israel, revealed that he "personally erased a key detail — that Hamas fighters were dressed as civilians and being counted as civilians in the death toll — because of a threat to our reporter in Gaza." Today, major news organizations, including the BBC and Agence France-Presse, have a policy of not using the word "terrorist" to describe Hamas terrorists — even those who committed atrocities on October 7th.

The Role of NGOs and Activists

Non-governmental organizations (NGOs) and activists also play a significant role in spreading biased narratives about Israel. For example, Amnesty International has been known to produce reports that are highly critical of Israel while downplaying or completely ignoring the actions of Hamas and other terrorist organizations. In one instance, Amnesty International referred to a 62-year-old terrorist, who had ordered the torture and murder of an Israeli soldier, simply as a "writer" and mourned his death without mentioning his crimes.

NGOs have invested heavily in their media wings, hiring communication professionals to build networks of contacts and influence public opinion. This has led to a shift toward "activist journalism," in which media organizations rely on reports from biased NGOs to shape their coverage. This spreads the manipulated truths exponentially and fuels anti-Israel opinions and beliefs.

Confronting the Big Lies

The persistence of big lies and manipulated truths about Jews and Israel throughout the history of the Jewish people and until the present day underscores the need for vigilance and proactive measures to counteract these falsehoods. Education, accurate reporting, and the promotion of truthful narratives are crucial in combating antisemitism and ensuring that history does not repeat itself. By understanding the origins and evolution of these lies, we can better equip ourselves to challenge them and promote a more informed and just perspective on the Jewish people and the state of Israel.

To counter these lies effectively, individuals and organizations must take active steps to confront misinformation. This includes supporting initiatives that work to correct biased reporting and provide accurate information about Israel and the history of the region, as well as fostering open and honest dialogue about the complexities of the Israeli-Palestinian conflict, which can help to dispel myths and promote a more nuanced understanding of the issues at hand.

The fight against antisemitism and the big lies about Jews and Israel is ongoing. It requires the collective efforts of individuals, communities, and institutions to stand up for truth and justice, ensuring that the lessons of history are remembered and that the rights and dignity of all people are upheld.

The Delusional Version of Events: Unmasking the October 7th Propaganda

Moshe Kaplan, MD

The Hamas terrorists' massacre in Israel on October 7th has been a focal point of global news coverage, generating a maelstrom of narratives. Although the horrific events of that day are undeniable, the way that the media and other organizations have since portrayed those events has often been riddled with inaccuracies, deliberate distortions, and outright falsehoods. Let us dissect some of the more delusional versions of these events, and juxtapose them against the factual accounts, to reveal the manipulation and propaganda at play.

Denial of the Mass Rape Perpetrated by the Hamas Barbarians

One of the most egregious lies that emerged in the aftermath of the October 7th massacre was the denial of the barbaric mass rapes that the Hamas terrorists committed against Israeli women. Ali Abunimah of *The Electronic Intifada*, contradicting clear evidence, wrote that the story of mass rapes was an "Israeli propaganda campaign." He claimed that the purpose was to propagate racist stereotypes that dehumanize Palestinians. Despite the piles of bodies, painstakingly collected forensic evidence, video footage from the terrorists themselves, as well statements from survivors and eyewitnesses, Abunimah professed to expose the Israeli fraud, claiming that no specific victims were identified, and that no forensic evidence or videos corroborated the claims!

He also contended that the "Civil Commission on October 7 Crimes by Hamas Against Women and Children," chaired by Dr. Cochav Elkayam-Levy, does not exist in any official capacity and has failed to produce a comprehensive report on the alleged crimes.

Manipulation of Casualty Figures

Hamas has been systematically manipulating casualty figures to paint Israel as the aggressor. The Hamas-run Ministry of Health in Gaza frequently reports inflated numbers of civilian casualties, particularly of women and children, to garner international sympathy and condemnation of Israel. According to analysts such as Abraham Wyner, a professor of statistics at the Wharton School, the casualty figures that Hamas has reported are statistically impossible — with an unrealistic proportion of women and children among the dead. One can only conclude the statistical anomalies in the Hamas reports point to deliberate manipulation of the numbers.

A study from the Washington Institute for Near East Policy highlights these discrepancies, finding significant inconsistencies in the reported numbers. It noted that on several occasions, the number of reported casualties fluctuated inexplicably, suggesting a lack of accurate data and a propensity for Hamas to manipulate figures to serve its narrative.

The UN's Role in Propagating Misinformation

The United Nations has frequently quoted Hamas-provided casualty figures, treating them as credible despite their dubious origins. This has led to a widespread acceptance of inflated and manipulated statistics, furthering the narrative of Israel as the primary aggressor. Many have criticized the UN's reliance on these figures because of its lack of scrutiny and its failure to verify the numbers independently, which has contributed to the spread of misinformation.

The Myth of the Mass Grave at Nassar Hospital

Another major falsehood that Hamas propagated was the claim about the contents of a mass grave discovered outside Nassar Hospital in Gaza, which allegedly containing bodies of Palestinians killed by Israeli forces. Major news outlets quickly picked up this story, which even prompted concern from U.S. officials. However, dated satellite video evidence that the Israeli army provided showed that Gazans had dug, filled, and closed the grave months earlier. This incident is a clear example of how Hamas fabricates stories to demonize Israel and manipulate public opinion.

The Happy Hostages Hoax

Hamas also falsely claimed that Israeli hostages released from captivity were "happy and laughing," having received generous treatment from their captors. This narrative was contradicted by the testimonies of the released hostages, who described horrific conditions, including starvation; confinement in dark, airless tunnels; and physical, emotional, and sexual abuse. The manipulation of hostage experiences for propaganda purposes underscores the lengths to which Hamas will go to present itself as humane while vilifying Israel.

Amnesty International's Misguided Reports

Amnesty International has also played a role in spreading misleading information about Israel's military actions. The organization has accused Israel of committing war crimes. These reports have been criticized for their lack of accuracy and for perpetuating a narrative that unfairly targets Israel while ignoring the complexities of the conflict and the actions of Hamas — most significantly its use of civilians as human shields, putting them in harm's way.

The BIG Truths: Israel's Sense of Moral Responsibility

Moshe Kaplan, MD

IN STARK CONTRAST to the twisted strategies of Hamas, Israel's actions reflect a profound sense of moral responsibility both to its own people and to humanity at large.

Israel goes to great lengths to minimize civilian casualties during its military operations. Prime Minister Benjamin Netanyahu highlighted how the IDF uses leaflets, text messages, and phone calls to warn civilians of impending strikes, allowing them to evacuate and stay safe. This effort is unprecedented in urban warfare and showcases Israel's commitment to humanitarian principles.

Israel actively provides humanitarian aid, even to those in enemy territories. Organizations like COGAT, working with the IDF, distribute food to displaced families, hostages, and orphans, ensuring they have what they need during difficult times. Such efforts highlight Israel's dedication to helping those in need, regardless of where they stand in the conflict.

Israel's medical teams, including the renowned IDF medical corps, often set up field hospitals and provide medical care to Palestinian civilians and fighters alike. This commitment to saving lives, even those of its adversaries, underscores the country's ethical stance in warfare and humanitarian aid.

Israel supports educational programs that promote peace and coexistence. These initiatives aim to counteract the indoctrination and hatred that groups like Hamas propagate and foster a new generation that values life and mutual respect.

Israeli government spokesperson, Avi Hyman, has states that although the IDF has killed more than 14,000 terrorists, it has maintained historically low civilian casualties, despite Hamas's active attempts to engage in fighting in civilian areas, using Gazan civilians as human shields. This statistic reflects Israel's strategy of precision targeting and its ethical approach to warfare, striving to set a new standard in conflict zones.

Israel's Efforts to Counteract Hamas's Propaganda

Israel has employed various strategies to combat Hamas's manipulation of reality.

Israel has launched numerous campaigns to highlight its humanitarian efforts and the moral and tactical complexities of the war. This includes showcasing the IDF's warnings to civilians before strikes and the provision of medical and humanitarian aid to Palestinians.

Recognizing the power of social media, Israel has ramped up its online presence, providing real-time updates, countering false claims, and sharing videos and evidence that refute Hamas's allegations. In this way, Israel aims to correct misinformation and present its perspective to a global audience.

Israel engages in legal and diplomatic channels to hold Hamas accountable for its actions. These efforts aim to educate foreign governments and international organizations about the realities of the war.

Despite these efforts, Israel still encounters significant hurdles in its battle against Hamas's propaganda. Many international media outlets seem to have a bias against Israel, often reporting Palestinian casualties without context or failing to highlight Hamas's provocations and tactics. This biased coverage makes it difficult for Israel to control the narrative.

The ingrained perception of Israel as a powerful state oppressing a weaker people is hard to shift. Emotional narratives tend to resonate more deeply with the public than factual counterarguments, thereby complicating Israel's efforts to alter public opinion.

The polarized political climate in many Western countries means that opinions on the Israeli-Palestinian conflict are often tied to broader ideological beliefs. This polarization makes objective analysis challenging, further clashing with Israel's counter-narrative efforts.

Chapter Three

The Silent Cry — Hamasticide (Apocalyptic Barbarism)

"Those who make peaceful revolution impossible, will make violent revolution inevitable"
— John F. Kennedy

Civilization versus Barbarism: An Irreconcilable Clash?

Moshe Kaplan, MD

For civilized people, a civilian death is a tragedy. For Hamas it is a strategy. Hamas is willing to let Gaza's residents die so that the international media will pressure Israel to end the war before it is won.

This would allow Hamas to survive to carry out October 7th again and again and again.

Anyone who believes in humanity doesn't want this to happen. But the voices of those who are moral and civilized are difficult to hear, despite the world's overwhelming silence in the face of the abuse of Jewish women and the destruction of Jewish lives.

Defeating a brutal enemy demands both courage and moral clarity. Clarity requires an understanding of the difference between good and evil. One would think that this would be clear. Yet many choose to stand with evil — with the Hamas barbarians, rapists, murderers — with terrorists who invaded the kibbutzim, smashed their way into people's homes, and murdered babies.

These supporters make no distinction between those

who target terrorists and those who target civilians. Students on campuses across the world chant "from the river to the sea," without knowing which river or which sea they mean. Even at top academic institutions in the USA, where students should be capable of evaluating facts to determine truth versus fiction, a false narrative and unbelievable ignorance held sway.

There is no moral leadership, as the people who run these campuses also seem not to know right from wrong. Eighty years after the Holocaust, the Presidents of Harvard, Penn, and MIT did not condemn the calls for the genocide of Jewish students. They said, "It depends on the context."

This is how supposedly intelligent people in the so-called civilized world justify, rationalize, accept, and promote the sick apocalyptic barbaric ideology and behavior of Hamas: Hamasticide.

So, we must ask: Is the civilized world civilized? Does it have a moral compass, a moral backbone? What does this mean for the future of humanity?

Under the influence of the existential movement and radical woke ideology, the Western/civilized world has moved away from moral accountability and responsibility, and toward increasing decadence. This is associated with increased crime, unrestrained use of psychotropic substances, and deviant behavior, both socially and sexually.

The decline undercuts the basis of Western civilization and has created a framework that allows uncivilized behavior to gain acceptance, blurring the distinction between civilization and barbarism. Current events clearly demonstrate that humanity has taken a turn for the worse.

We need to face the fact that October 7th's objectification of women's bodies, weaponization of sexual assault, and rape in warfare has brought the human race to a new low.

Civilization is failing the hostages right now, and it is failing all of humanity.

Until there is enough public outrage, until the world cries out, demanding the destruction of the Hamas barbarians and the release of the hostages, the world cannot be at peace. People of moral turpitude must work relentlessly to keep the soul of the world from disintegrating.

Setting Things Straight — Hamas Are Not "Militants," They're Terrorists!

Nils A. Haug

"Israel has implemented more precautions to prevent civilian harm than any military in history- above and beyond what international law requires and more than the US did in its wars in Iraq and Afghanistan."
—John Spencer, Chairman of Urban Warfare Studies at West Point

Contrasting Ideologies: The Stark Differences between the IDF and Hamas

Hamas, the Palestinian Islamic organization, operates in a deeply sinister and criminal manner, as various accounts and reports have vividly illustrated. Its *modus operandus* is a blend of extreme violence, strategic manipulation of civilian spaces, and the exploitation of humanitarian resources, which collectively paint a disturbing picture of the organization's activities.

Take, for instance, the confession of a Gazan terrorist affiliated with the Palestinian Islamic Jihad movement. During an interrogation by Israeli forces, Manar Mahmoud

Muhammad Kasem described, in gruesome detail, his actions during the invasion of October 7th. Kasem admitted to crossing the Israel-Gaza border armed with a pistol and grenades, and said that during a chaotic encounter, he entered a kibbutz and raped an Israeli woman in her home. His candid recounting reveals not just a personal depravity but also a chilling example of the kind of terror Hamas and its affiliates instill in their victims. Unfortunately, this disturbing incident was not isolated.

This utter lack of respect for life and the living ties to a broader pattern of behavior in which Hamas systematically uses civilian and humanitarian spaces for their operations. For instance, Israeli Defense Forces (IDF) uncovered a massive cache of weapons in the maternity ward of Shifa Hospital in Gaza City. This included mortar shells, explosive devices, and firearms, all strategically hidden within the hospital, putting patients and medical staff at severe risk. Such actions blatantly violate international laws and conventions, which prioritize the safety of medical facilities and their occupants.

Hamas's exploitation of civilian infrastructure extends beyond hospitals. The IDF also reported that Hamas utilized a United Nations Relief and Works Agency (UNRWA) compound as a base for their operations. This included a command-and-control center within the UNRWA compound, from which Hamas orchestrated attacks on Israeli troops and disrupted the distribution of humanitarian aid. This misuse of UN facilities not only endangers civilians seeking refuge, but also undermines the integrity and mission of international humanitarian organizations.

The use of civilians as human shields is another hallmark of Hamas's tactics. During an operation in Beit

Hanoun, Israeli forces encountered Hamas and Palestinian Islamic Jihad terrorists who were using a school as cover. Despite the presence of civilians, these terrorists were willing to engage in combat, further jeopardizing the lives of innocent bystanders. This strategic placement of military operations in civilian areas serves to both shield Hamas fighters from retaliation and to provoke international outrage against any defensive actions that Israel takes.

The manipulation and theft of humanitarian aid is another critical aspect of Hamas's operations. Reports have surfaced detailing the ways that Hamas diverts significant portions of aid meant for Gaza's civilian population. For example, Hamas fighters often hijack aid trucks and food supplies, leading to severe shortages and inflated prices for basic goods in Gaza. Hamas's hoarding and resale of aid not only creates artificial scarcity but also lines the pockets of Hamas leaders, further entrenching their power at the expense of the very people they claim to represent.

Hamas's control over financial resources extends to even the most basic amenities. In a particularly egregious example, Hamas has taken control of ATMs in Gaza, restricting ordinary citizens' access to cash and ensuring that only those aligned with their interests can withdraw money. This kind of financial manipulation exacerbates the economic hardship that Gaza's residents face and consolidates Hamas's grip over the territory.

Internationally, Hamas's connections and their support of the organization are of concern. Iranian involvement in planning and executing terrorist operations highlights a broader network of state-supported terrorism. Having Iran's backing relationship emboldens

Hamas and enables it to engage in more sophisticated and destructive operations, such as the October 7th attack. Iran's technical expertise, weapons, and financial resources make Hamas a more formidable adversary than it would be on its own. Hamas's relationship with Iran not only gives the organization strategic and financial support, but also aligns it with other extremist ideologies, further complicating the geopolitical landscape.

In stark contrast to the actions of Hamas, the Israeli Defense Forces (IDF) exhibit a humane, moral approach, particularly in their treatment of civilians, and their humanitarian efforts. The IDF operates under a strict code of ethics that emphasizes the protection of innocent lives, even during conflicts. For example, the IDF has gone to great lengths to warn Gaza civilians of impending attacks in order to minimize casualties. This includes phone calls, leaflets, and "roof knocking" — the firing of non-lethal warning shots on roofs before bombing — to ensure that civilians know that they should evacuate.

While Hamas has manipulated and stolen humanitarian aid, the IDF has taken significant steps to facilitate getting this aid to Gazans, despite the ongoing war with Hamas. One notable effort has been the establishment of humanitarian corridors, which allow for the safe passage of essential supplies to Gaza. The IDF has enabled the passage of over 1,200 aid trucks since the start of the war. These trucks have delivered more than 20,000 tons of humanitarian aid, including food, water, medical supplies, and other necessary goods to support the civilian population in Gaza.

These efforts are part of an initiative that Israel has meticulously coordinated with international organizations and humanitarian agencies, with the goal of getting aid to those who need it most, despite the ongoing war.

Additionally, the IDF has set up temporary ceasefires, known as humanitarian pauses, to allow aid to be delivered, and to enable civilians to escape conflict zones. These pauses are critical, as they provide a window of safety for aid workers, and facilitate the distribution of humanitarian assistance. Moreover, the IDF has facilitated the transport of injured Gazans to hospitals, including those in Israel, for treatment, highlighting the army's commitment to humanitarian principles despite the conflict. These efforts underscore the IDF's role in balancing military objectives with the need to mitigate the humanitarian impact on the civilian population in Gaza. This is in stark contrast to Hamas's strategy of endangering civilians and misappropriating humanitarian resources.

US Senator Lindsey Graham highlighted this difference by calling claims that Israel is starving Gazans "a modern-day blood libel." He noted that "never in the history of warfare have I seen such an effort by one of the protagonists in a war to lessen the effect on the population of the other side," emphasizing the Israeli military's efforts to ensure that innocent Palestinians receive the basics of life.

Understanding the ideological underpinnings of each side further accentuates these differences. Hamas's chief ideological document, its 1988 charter, calls for the "struggle against the Jews with all means and methods." This is not just a battle strategy but a foundational belief that drives its actions. This charter, along with its 2017 declaration, uses divine and international laws, as Hamas interprets them, to legitimize its use of violence and terror against Israel. This is reflected in the organization's battle ethics and practices, including using human shields, targeting civilians, and leveraging civilian suffering to gain international sympathy and support.

The IDF's "Purity of Arms" doctrine presents its guiding principles. This doctrine, which dates from the formation of the IDF, emphasizes the use of arms only when necessary and strictly for the fulfillment of the mission. The IDF's code, "The Spirit of the IDF," enshrines values such as human dignity, stating that all individuals have inherent value regardless of their background. The army's operational procedures, which aim to minimize civilian casualties and uphold the highest standards of human rights, even during intense military engagement, reflect this commitment.

Hamas's doctrine of indiscriminate cruelty and barbarism differs greatly from the IDF's approach. *The Warrior's Guide: Jihadi Version*, a manual recovered from a Hamas operative, outlines horrific tactics such as taking hostages, using electric shocks, gunfire, and grenades to control captives, and using them as human shields. The manual underscores the brutal reality of Hamas's operational ethics, which are deeply rooted in the organization's ideological commitment to the destruction of Israel and the extermination of Jews.

The contrasting doctrines and operational behaviors of the IDF and Hamas reveal a fundamental difference in their values and objectives. The IDF's commitment to human dignity and ethical warfare contrasts starkly with Hamas's ruthless and indiscriminate violence. This divergence highlights the asymmetric nature of the conflict, where one side strives to uphold international norms and protect civilians, while the other flagrantly violates these principles in pursuit of its destructive goals.

Gazan Perspectives: The Complex Views on Hamas and the October 7th Attack

The complex and often contradictory views of Palestinians in Gaza regarding Hamas leadership and the October 7th attack against Israel reveal a community deeply influenced by decades of conflict and the harsh realities of daily life under Hamas's rule. Hamas causes its citizens untold suffering and destruction, and yet the support for Hamas and its actions varies significantly among Gazans - reflecting a blend of fear, resilience, and desire for a better future.

On October 7th, Hamas launched a brutal attack on Israel, resulting in the deaths of 1,200 people, mostly civilians, and the abduction of over 250 individuals. Hamas accompanied the assault with heinous acts of violence, including mass rape, defiling and sexually violating the dead, beheadings, and torture. Despite the extent of these atrocities, a significant majority of Palestinians in Gaza and the West Bank support the attack. According to a poll that the Palestinian Center for Policy and Survey Research (PCPSR) conducted, 71% of Palestinians believe the decision to attack Israel was correct, and 93% do not believe that Hamas committed any atrocities during the invasion; even among those who watched videos of the atrocities, 81% did not believe that they had happened. This disconnect underscores the power of propaganda and the deep-seated mistrust in information perceived to be from external or opposing sources.

However, support for Hamas's leadership and tactics is not unilateral. Despite the general backing of the attack, there is growing criticism of Hamas within Gaza. The war has displaced a large portion of Gaza's population, led to the deaths of tens of thousands, and pushed the enclave toward the brink of famine. Many Gazans are frustrated with Hamas, blaming the militant group for the ongoing conflict and their deteriorating living conditions.

For instance, Salma El-Qadomi, a freelance journalist, expressed the opinion that Hamas should have secured a place of refuge for the people instead of plunging them into unbearable suffering. Similarly, Fedaa Zayed, a writer from northern Gaza, criticized Hamas for refusing ceasefire offers, suggesting that the group's reluctance to end the war stems from an unwillingness to admit defeat. These sentiments reflect a desire for peace and stability among some Gazans, who are weary of the continuous bloodshed and hardship.

The polling data reveal that while a slim majority in Gaza prefer Hamas to remain in control after the war, this preference might stem more from fear and resignation than from genuine support. Khalil Sayegh, a Palestinian political analyst, suggests that the people's expressed support for Hamas might reflect the fear of retribution and the perceived inevitability of Hamas's continued rule. Mkhaimar Abusada, a professor of political science, explains that Palestinians are wary of being perceived as collaborating with Israel if they protest against Hamas during the conflict. This internal tension highlights the complex dynamics of support and opposition within the Palestinian community.

In the broader context, the international response to the conflict and its portrayal of Hamas also plays a significant role in shaping opinions. The Western media's dissemination of Hamas's propaganda as facts has contributed to a skewed perception of the conflict, putting undue pressure on Israel while often glossing over

Hamas's culpability. This biased narrative has significant repercussions, because it influences public opinion and international policy.

A Double Standard: The World's Hypocritical Stance on Israel

The current war between Israel and Hamas has once again highlighted the glaring double standards to which the international community often subjects Israel. Despite its efforts to abide by international laws and prioritize the safety of civilians, Israel faces relentless criticism and unjust accusations. Meanwhile, global feminist organizations and the Western media often downplay or ignore Hamas's barbarism, particularly against Jewish, Israeli women during the October 7th attack. This essay delves into these double standards, providing examples of the bias and propaganda that unfairly target Israel.

The global narrative often sides with Hamas, disseminating its propaganda as facts. Many Western media outlets and international organizations quickly accept and spread Hamas's claims, putting undue pressure on Israel. US Secretary of State Antony Blinken condemned the violence but also questioned the slow response from international bodies, suggesting that ideological biases might be at work.

The willingness of the global population to accept Hamas's propaganda is troubling. Jared Kushner, in a piece for Townhall.com, criticized organizations supporting LGBT rights for condemning Israel — a country that grants freedom — while marching in support of Hamas, a group that punishes gay people with death.

A striking example of this double standard appears in the response to humanitarian efforts. Despite Israel's diligent efforts to ensure the flow of aid into Gaza, it faces baseless accusations of causing famine. US Defense Secretary Lloyd Austin firmly rejected claims that Israel is committing genocide, pointing out that no evidence supports such accusations. White House spokesman John Kirby echoed this, stating that US investigations found no instances in which Israel has violated international humanitarian law.

In contrast, reports consistently show that Hamas manipulates and hoards humanitarian aid, creating artificial scarcity in order to garner international sympathy. Veteran journalist Alon Goldstein addressed the Biden administration, stressing that "there's no famine in Gaza" and highlighting how Hamas's opportunism inflates prices and perpetuates suffering. Despite these facts, the narrative of Israel as the oppressor persists, often fueled by biased media coverage and political agendas.

The hypocrisy is further evident in feminist organizations' responses, or lack thereof, to the October 7th atrocities. These groups, which should be at the forefront of condemning such violence, have largely remained silent. Reem Alsalem, the United Nations' Special Rapporteur on Violence Against Women and Girls, asserted that the evidence against Hamas wasn't solid enough for a formal statement, despite overwhelming evidence to the contrary. Her stance prompted Claire Waxman, London's Victims' Commissioner, to question the UN's commitment to eliminating violence against women, since it appears that Jewish women can be attacked without condemnation.

The International Day for the Elimination of Violence against Women passed without mention of the attacks on Israeli women. Figures like Sheryl Sandberg and Senator Kirsten Gillibrand spoke out against Hamas's crimes, but only in March 2024 did the UN acknowledge the sexual violence that Hamas had perpetrated. Even then, it took no significant action, such as declaring Hamas a terror group.

This double standard is deeply rooted in ideological biases and a reluctance to challenge the dominant narrative. Radical feminist groups often deflect criticism, blaming Israel for discrediting feminists rather than condemning Hamas's actions. This aligns with a broader Marxian class-dualist theory, which views Palestinians as oppressed and therefore justifies their actions against Israelis.

This double standard to which Israel is held is stark and pervasive. Despite its efforts to minimize civilian casualties and provide humanitarian aid, Israel faces relentless criticism and unfounded accusations. Meanwhile, the world often ignores or downplays Hamas's atrocities, particularly against women. This hypocrisy undermines the principles of justice and equality, and it perpetuates a biased and distorted narrative. It is crucial to address these double standards and to hold all parties accountable for their actions, ensuring a fair and truthful representation of the conflict.

Inside Hamas: How the Terrorist Organization Uses Guerrilla Tactics to Wage War

Darcie Grunblatt for the Jerusalem Post, July 13, 2024

Hamas fighters dress as civilians, store weapons in civilian homes, in mosques, in the linings of sofas, and in the walls of children's bedrooms, and they hide beneath the ground in an extensive network of tunnels, the *New York Times* reported Saturday in an extensive expose of Hamas's use of guerrilla warfare.

Throughout over eight months of fighting in Gaza, the Qassam Brigades have fought as a primarily hidden force, only briefly emerging from underground tunnels, occasionally, grenade in hand, to kill soldiers. Hamas forces have largely abandoned their bases and outposts to overcome Israel's technological and numerical advantages by launching surprise attacks on small squads of soldiers, the *Times* reported.

The *New York Times* conducted its analysis using Hamas-released battlefield videos, interviews with three Hamas members, and interviews with many Israeli soldiers, most of whom spoke to the *Times* on the condition of anonymity because they were not permitted to speak publicly.

Based on these sources, the *Times* concluded that Hamas's strategy of hiding includes using hundreds of miles of tunnels to move around Gaza without being seen by Israeli soldiers and using civilian homes and infrastructure, including medical facilities, UN facilities, and mosques, to conceal fighters, tunnel entrances, booby-traps, and ammunition stores.

Its tactics include ambushing Israeli soldiers with small groups of fighters dressed as civilians, as well as using civilians, including children, to act as lookouts, leaving secret signals outside homes, like a red sheet hanging from a window or graffiti, to tell fellow fighters the nearby presence of mines, tunnel entrances, or weapons inside.

Additionally, another strategy used is to drag the war out for as long as possible, even at the expense of more civilian death and destruction, to exhaust Israel in an attritional battle that has increased international condemnation of Israel.

In an interview with the *Times*, a member of Hamas, Salah al-Din al-Awawdeh, said, "The aim is to vanish, avoid direct confrontation while launching tactical attacks against the occupation army. The emphasis is on patience."

Before October 7, the Qassam Brigades operated as "an army with training bases and stockpiles," al-Awawdeh said. "But during this war, they are behaving as guerrillas," he shared.

At the beginning of the war, Hamas and its local allies fired a barrage of rockets toward civilian areas of Israel, using launchers based in densely populated civilian areas of Gaza. The IDF captured and destroyed these launchers, which they found near a mosque and a kindergarten.

The *Times* report also included a statement by a senior Hamas official based in Qatar, who defended the use of these tactics and claimed that condemning these tactics distracted from paying attention to Israeli wrongdoing.

"If there's someone who takes a weapon from under a bed, is that a justification for killing 100,000 people?" Mousa Abu Marzouk said. "If someone takes a weapon from under a bed, is that a justification to kill an entire school and destroy a hospital?" Although Marzouk alludes to Hamas operatives performing these actions by chance, the extensiveness of these activities illustrates that storing weapons in civilian homes is a plan and a strategy for the war.

"Every insurgency in every war, from Vietnam to Afghanistan, saw people fighting from their homes," said Hamas member al-Awawdeh. "If I live in Zeitoun, for example, and the army comes — I will fight them there, from my home, or my neighbor's, or from the mosque. I will fight them anywhere I am."

Hamas fighters wear civilian clothes in a legitimate attempt to avoid detection, al-Awawdeh added. "That's natural for a resistance movement," he said, "and there's nothing unusual about it."

According to International Law and the rules of war, since civilians are not lawful objects of attack in armed conflict, it follows that disguising combatants in civilian clothing to commit hostilities constitutes perfidy. An act of perfidy occurs when someone uses the protective provisions of the Geneva Conventions with the intention of deceiving, killing, injuring, or capturing an opponent.

Using residential buildings, civilian homes for stockpiling weaponry

Hamas has also used residential buildings to hide weaponry throughout the Strip, the *Times* reported, citing over a dozen Israeli soldiers who found these weapon stockpiles.

The soldiers said it became customary to find munitions hidden inside civilian homes and mosques.

Some soldiers said their units needlessly destroyed civilian property, but others said there was usually a military purpose for going through civilian belongings. According to the *Times*, one soldier found guns behind a false wall in a child's bedroom, and another said they found grenades in a woman's clothing closet.

When Gazans began to evacuate in October, Hamas terrorists began booby-trapping hundreds of houses, the *Times* reported, citing the Hamas official. The mines were linked to tripwires, movement sensors, and sound detectors that detonate the explosives once triggered. After this, the terrorists went into the tunnels.

International law requires combatants to avoid using "civilian objects," which include homes, schools, hospitals, and mosques, for military objectives.

To help fellow Hamas members find these weapons caches inside civilian homes, several Israeli soldiers said, Hamas has developed a system of code for marking houses that contain weapons, tunnels, or booby traps.

Some Israeli units were given printed guides to help them identify the meaning of each symbol or object used to mark homes, a soldier told the *Times*.

Soldiers sometimes entered houses by blowing a hole in their walls in case the front doors were rigged with mines, according to a senior military officer, Maj. Gen. Itai Veruv.

To draw Israelis toward a trap, Hamas members sometimes scattered a building with visible signs of their presence, such as a Hamas flag. At other times, two Israeli soldiers said, Israeli troops were lured inside by a piece of Israeli clothing or identification card, which hinted that hostages might be held inside.

One soldier said Hamas used chained dogs to entrap IDF soldiers in a rigged building, hoping that the soldiers would try to free the dogs.

Another soldier spotted a dead Hamas fighter inside an apartment block and made his way toward the body. As he came closer, he realized the corpse had been rigged with an explosive, he said. When his squad fired at the body, it blew up and set the building ablaze, he said.

Ambushing Israeli soldiers

When soldiers first invaded Gaza, they were not met with Hamas fighters at their bases or outposts. According to a Hamas fighter, this was because the Qassam Brigades' strategy was to ambush Israeli soldiers once they had advanced deep into the territory.

There are videos across social media that display Hamas fighters in civilian clothes emerging from tunnels to attack Israeli tanks, attaching mines near the turrets of the tanks, firing rocket-propelled grenades from residential buildings, and shooting at soldiers with sniper rifles.

Hamas had been preparing for a ground war since at least 2021, when the group began scaling up production of explosives and anti-tank missiles and stopped making so many long-range rockets, the Hamas officer said.

It also prepared by increasing the number of tunnels across the territory, fitted with a landline telephone network that is difficult for Israel to monitor and permits the terrorists to communicate even during outages to Gaza's mobile phone networks, which are controlled by

Israel, according to the Hamas officer, al-Awawdeh, and Israeli officials.

According to the *Times* report, Hamas has enough food rations in the tunnels for at least ten months, and the terrorists have trained themselves to consume as little rations as possible and still be able to remain focused.

In well-planned ambushes, Hamas squads allow Israeli soldiers to roam freely for hours or even days in areas marked for attack. They track the IDF soldiers' locations using hidden cameras, drones, and intelligence provided by civilian lookouts, including children, according to five Israeli soldiers. They said the children stand on roofs and provide information to commanders below.

The terrorists stay hidden until an Israeli convoy has moved through one area for several minutes or Israeli forces have grouped in a particular place for hours, so they believed Hamas had left the area. After a period of calm, a group of four terrorists will emerge from the tunnels.

Two of them attach explosives to the sides of a vehicle or fire anti-tank missiles at it. A third carries a camera to film propaganda footage, and the fourth stays at the tunnel entrance to prepare a booby-trap that will be activated when the others return, to kill any Israelis who try to enter the tunnel.

The terrorist squads aim to take out not only the initial Israeli force but also the backup fighters and medics who come to rescue the wounded, the *Times* reported, citing the Hamas officer as well as Israeli soldiers who experienced such ambushes.

These tactics have been videographed by Hamas and appear in an extensive eight-minute video released on its social media channels in early April.

In the video that is inaccessible to *The Jerusalem Post*, Hamas operatives planned an attack using pen, paper, and a digital tablet to draw maps of where they wanted to plant roadside mines. "We ask, O Lord, for the ambush to achieve its goals — let us kill your enemies, the Jews," the narrator of the video says, according to the *Times*.

Next, Hamas terrorists, wearing civilian clothes, are seen laying those explosives in the rubble of a ruined neighborhood. Then, the video cuts to what appears to be the planned ambush. A group of Israeli soldiers making their way through the rubble were hit by gunfire. That attack brought an Israeli relief squad to the scene, and the arrival of those rescuers appeared to trigger the laid-out mines. This footage was taken by hidden cameras in the area.

"This is a miniature sample of what their defeated army is suffering in the mire of Gaza," the narrator concluded in the video.

Hamasticide: Apocalyptic Barbarians at the Gates of Israel

Fiamma Nierenstein

The Descent into Barbarism in the World

It was the morning of October 7, 2023. The sun shone gloriously on the yellow sand, the grass of the kibbutzim, the swing chairs beneath the veranda, the lopsided sculptures, the children's bicycles, the grandparents' electric cars, the shells threaded onto string swinging in the wind and tinkling in front of the houses. The sea nearby. Everyone was sleeping.

It was six o'clock on Shabbat morning. Not far away, a crowd of thousands of young people had been dancing to pounding rave music at a festival called Nova, lightheaded with youth and peace until collapsing into sleep.

In the kibbutzim of southern Israel, this was the beginning of a holiday; nobody knew of the reality of roaring white pickup trucks breaking through the mesh fences and walls to invade. The inhabitants of Be'eri or Kfar Aza had wanted to create in the south one of the most utopian pictures of the homeland of the Jewish people, in the style of the early twenty-first century: a little socialist, very loving, ecological, and pacifist, as well as technological, even holding a daily dialogue with the inhabitants of Gaza, their neighbors across the yellow space, with gifts to the children, cookies, and health care.

At six-thirty, the legion of children, about three per family, princes and princesses, masters of all, were sleeping before a new royal awakening of kisses and cookies. The grandparents had left the Friday-night tables half laid, with the traces of the large families who had eaten the foods of their Polish or Moroccan past. They would sleep a little longer, as would the longhaired post-army youngsters, with the guitars propped in the corner, the cell phones already buzzing with all the TikToks trying vainly to warn them: "Wake up, something's going on!" But it was too late. In the houses overflowing with books and flowers, the many peace ideals would be incinerated with special thermobaric RPG grenades, large black spindles (we saw dozens of unexploded ones) that explode at 2000 degrees and carbonize everything, leaving the victims and the houses, objects, and people, unrecognizable and unidentifiable. This is precisely what happened. I have seen photographs of the carbonized victims, like the victims of Pompeii.

As missiles began to rain everywhere, much more than the usual barrage of constant Hamas shells, I received a call from my shocked friend Ruthie: "Do you maybe know why they're shooting so much and everywhere?" I didn't know, nobody knew, nobody was expecting it. As in 1973, when the Yom Kippur War took a toll of about 2,700 Israeli soldiers, Israel had believed that its moral and technological superiority, its mythical powers of survival against all and everything, nullified any warning, any forecast. Instead, everything would soon be ashes and blood.

In the 1920s and 1930s, in Europe, Gershom Scholem, Franz Rosenzweig, Walter Benjamin, and others relied on the refinement of advanced German thought without an inkling that anything was brewing in the country. They did not know, precisely because of their sophistication and hope in life joined with materialization, that a monster was lurking in the shadows, planning how to kill all the Jews, one by one, and bury them under the ruins of Europe.

Thus, Be'eri rested until 6:30, among the sweetest Israeli dreams. It is one of the border kibbutzim known for its pacifism, for seeking a secular *tikkun olam*, a mending of the world where man helps G-d to complete the Creation. But then, the truth had only one color, that of Jewish blood, and the pogrom arrived on pickup trucks.

Batya Holin of Kibbutz Kfar Aza, who had prepared with five Gazan photographers a very successful joint exhibition, noted that four of them had disappeared in the days before the massacre. During the killings, the fifth phoned her from within the border, where he had broken in with the monsters, asking her where she was, if there were soldiers around them, and if she was with her whole family. "He was digging for information," Batya said. "Only then, while they were trying to break into our hiding place, did I understand that he was a terrorist."

To believe that what happened is true, I had to watch, several times over, the footage that the Hamas operatives collected with their video cameras. I had to listen and listen again to a hundred horror stories, visit the ruins, meet the survivors... and it is still hard to believe with my own eyes and my own ears. In the shadows of the tunnels under the buildings in Gaza or up and down the no-man's-land between Gaza and Israel, the Hamas men had been given careful training and detailed instructions for months. Their preparations, like those of the Syrians and Egyptians for the surprise attack of 1973, were not secret: Hamas leaders held meetings and distributed leaflets with instructions and maps. The orders were: "While rockets are being launched from here [Gaza] and they are all taking refuge in their homes, invade, kill, rape, tear them apart, burn them, cut off heads and limbs." Whose? Everyone's — babies, mothers, children, older people, young men and women. And to take into captivity in Gaza a most diverse sections of Jews, so that the blackmail would affect all of Israeli society.

Hamas leader, Yahya Sinwar, used his imagination well, ordering the tearing of children from their mothers' arms and the killing of mothers in front of their children, inventing every possible way to make the terror more horrendous than that of ISIS, to exterminate in the cruelest manner possible. Sinwar commanded his men to kill babies, brutally rape women of any age, even girls, whether alive or dead; to castrate men and boys; to decapitate; to burn entire families alive together along with the symbols of their lives. Thus, he forever epitomized the savagery of his movement, making him the absolute leader of contemporary hatred. Sinwar placed Hamas at the head of a worldwide movement for the deconstruction of history that legitimizes rage as the emblem of life. That believes that it must take this action against all of civilization. This movement has decided that the contemporary outcome of history and religion, including the Jewish-Christian civilization and the human rights culture, is advantageous only for those who created it, and so it is a tool of oppression to be ripped to pieces. The diabolical choice to tear down this civilization permits any means to destroy the "colonialists," the "imperialists," the "racists," the rich, the white men, and above all, of course, the Jews.

This concept finds consensus far from Gaza, first in the Muslim world, which places the "Islamophobes" among the oppressors, and along with the students, the LGTBQ movements, the ecological movements that think the earth will be destroyed by capitalist interests, and the Jews. The UN, the Palestinian Authority, and even the Ivy League universities have still not condemned Sinwar's atrocities. It is a crime whose "context" is what counts, and nobody expected that after a massacre like October 7, the destruction of contemporary civilization would piggyback on an antisemitic atrocity.

The plan, unlike that of the Nazis in their time, was to destroy the Jews by publicizing as widely as possible the resolve to make them suffer one by one. Hamas leaders repeated the promise: "We did it, and we will do it again and again and again."

Once the barbarians entered Israel, they roared down the roads by the hundreds in white pickup trucks and on motorbikes, shooting everyone they encountered, pedestrians and drivers, in the head, and chasing those who tried to escape. They were divided into units, some assigned to close public roads, while others headed for the countryside and the kibbutzim. They were systematic, coming back to seize anyone who might have escaped them. They opened the doors of the cars abandoned at the sides of the roads to make sure everyone was dead and to finish off the wounded. Then they came together to shout for joy over the bodies of the dead: "*Itbah el Yehud! Allah hu Akbar!*"

They all shouted with the index finger raised, indicating

their blasphemous oneness of G-d, the primal call of jihadism: Allah is great. By cutting off the head of a baby, the murderer was fulfilling the mission of reconquering the land occupied by the Jews, purifying it of the Western and democratic culture. "*Yehud, Yehud!*" alerted the comrades to the next victims. Advancing over the green fields of the kibbutzim, they sought out anyone in hiding. When they entered the houses of the kibbutzim, they slaughtered a grandmother hugging two children. When they saw a hero, and there were so many, coming out with a gun in hand to try to stop them, they exclaimed, "*Yehud!*" Then they would slit his throat and burn him. One killer was recorded phoning his mother in Gaza to brag he had killed ten Jews. This is what he and his colleagues had learned at school from an early age, based on the Hamas Charter. *Yehud* is, according to the Islamic texts, a lowly being, a "son of pigs and monkeys," just as Hitler's *juden* were considered roaches — destined for slaughter because they are not human.

Each Hamas team headed for a kibbutz, and in the kibbutzim, they searched house by house for the families, then killed them in the most unthinkable ways, concentrating on the children. The terrorists had maps that they had developed after working in the communities. They knew who lived where, how many they were, and where the children's bedrooms were.

As filmed by the murderers' own cameras affixed to their foreheads, I saw their house-by-house hunt, the pursuit of the children, and the discovery of desperate families huddled in their safe rooms. The monsters in the videos walked on the green lawns with their machine guns drawn, searched in small groups for their next victims, threw hand grenades, broke down doors, and found yet another one, two, three people stupefied by their encounter with death, then killed the family. Ten against one, they encountered a desperate father coming out to defend his family or an unsuspecting and heroic cop who had rushed to answer the call.

In the films, you see how they went into the houses, searched out people to be killed, and fired on the children and the families in their rooms and beds. You see a Thai man hacked to death with an ax. Two children, together with their father, dash for the shelter of their home, but a grenade slaughters the father. The children, hurled to one side, are crying, one of them no longer able to see out of one eye. The older boy, about eight, hugs and tries to comfort the younger one, who must be about five, asking him if he can see but telling him not to call "Abba" (Daddy); Abba is really dead, unlike in the cartoons. I have no idea what happened to them. Other stories of unspeakable cruelties and glorious courage in fighting, resisting, and dying on behalf of others now form a tapestry, and who knows when we will finish weaving it? Human body parts are still being found, and confirmations of the definitive loss of somebody missing and not abducted are still emerging. As I write, another two people thought to have been kidnapped were found to have been murdered. There are so many whose bodies are in no state even for burial because the phosphorus bombs reduced the bodies to a handful of charcoal. Saintly volunteers are still searching for a sign the survivors can recognize: a ring, sometimes an earring, a polished nail.

There are stories of the carbonized dead killed inside the safe rooms; there were always members of the family who, taking turns, tried to secure the door handle until the terrorists succeeded in smashing the door or the window. The last phone calls to the relatives say, "They're in the house, goodbye, I love you." Then, as communication is cut off, the monsters smash open the doors and, with their automatic weapons, kill all the families, piling bodies on the floor or in the beds in lakes of blood. Or they burn everything with the hand grenades and the flamethrowers, shouting with joy amid the orgy, displaying the results to each other. If they did not manage to get into the shelters, they searched for a window through which to toss in a bomb that would incinerate the closed space, leaving only unrecognizable bodies and objects, black shadows with grimaces like those of Pompeii. Sometimes, the victims died of asphyxiation, especially the children. A baby was saved because he was held on the windowsill to breathe the air, on and off, for about ten hours. Children aged four and five stayed quiet in their hiding places for twelve hours, petrified.

The siege lasted for over twelve hours. The rescuers who arrived at the beginning were few — lightly armed and altruistic policemen, soldiers on leave who did not know what they would find. Often, the men of the family tried to defend the house with a weapon — a gun, a knife. Heroic soldiers who rushed in from outside, and without understanding what was happening, met their death in battle.

Meanwhile, the terrorists carried out and abducted stupefied and crying small children. Mothers bent over the bodies of infants were dragged away. The two little Bibas children, the redheaded baby and his brother, were abducted along with their weeping mother. Their fate is unknown. Babies and the elderly were hoisted onto motorbikes, women were forcibly stripped and thrown by the hair into cars, then filmed as they were fed to the ferocious mob in Gaza. The rapes cannot be counted; nor can the extent of the accompanying mutilations. The abducted women were now widows, the children were now orphans, the husbands were now bereft, and they had to face captivity.

Just beyond Kibbutz Be'eri, surging along the roads and dropping from the sky on hang glider wings, Hamas gunmen found the most convenient slaughter site: The Nova Festival, where one thousand young music lovers danced. They would kill three hundred of them. The footage shows the dancers running, desperate, with no escape. The music stops, and the incredulous screaming starts as the monsters' advance; smiles and song give way to rape and carnage. Mad with the joy of killing so many Jews at one time, the terrorists — some drug-fueled — shot, raped, beat, burned, and piled up the hundreds of dead and broken bodies like garbage that rescuers continue to find weeks after the massacre. Some survived by pretending to be dead, buried under the piles of their murdered friends. This is where most of the femicide occurred, leaving the bodies of the women piled, bloodstained, their lower parts bare and mutilated, and some with broken pelvic bones.

What happened on October 7 challenges the very question of what it is to be a human being. Perhaps for this reason, the world inverted an event of blinding clarity to the point of blaming the victims; we see the masochistic fate to which our civilization voluntarily surrenders itself, refusing to comprehend, to condemn, or to fight alongside Israel.

October 7 put before the intellectuals, the university campuses, the UN, and the European Union a unique opportunity for verification: the Jews were murdered mercilessly, and antisemitism cried out from the videos and the testimonies of the survivors. But suddenly, UN Secretary-General António Guterres proposed an explanation for all this — the lack of human rights, the occupation, the Palestinians who had suffered for the past 75 years, and the absence of two states for two peoples. "These are the reasons for this. It does not occur in a vacuum," said Guterres. The French president exhorted, "Israel, do not kill women and children," as if without this instruction, Israel would have done so. In reality, Israel is the only country that, in the course of a just war, takes care to warn the civilians on enemy territory of the dangers and to create humanitarian corridors for their flight. In contrast, Hamas fighters blocked their escape routes, so that they could use the Palestinians as human shields. They forced women and children to remain in the war zone as protection for the Hamas terrorists and the enormous quantities of weapons that the Israeli Army has discovered hidden in homes, mosques, hospitals, and schools. Gaza is one giant bunker filled with tunnels in which only Hamas fighters may take refuge, heedless of Gazan suffering. On the contrary, it is eager to sacrifice lives for its propaganda purposes.

With the slaughter of Jews in a corner of Israel came the wave of antisemitism across the globe — a veritable green light for genocide. We Jews are once again petrified. October 7 happened not long after I wrote "Jewish Lives Matter," which described the transition from human rights concerns to antisemitism. I had not anticipated the inflamed mobs searching for Jews all over the world. The same intellectual assumptions that prevented us from foreseeing what was brewing in Gaza blinded us to the tsunami of hatred against the Jews that poured over both Israel and the Jewish community worldwide, and with which we are now dealing. In 1973, too, the Yom Kippur War did not seem possible until it broke out, because we were still imbued with the victory of the Six-Day War; now, in postmodern Israeli ideology, nobody wanted to believe that a bloodthirsty medieval army would come stampeding across our border.

A few days after October 7th, in the squares of Europe and America, in Madrid, Paris, Rome, and New York, and on college campuses, demonstrators shouted: "Hamas, Hamas, kill the Jews!" waving Palestinian and Hamas flags. They chanted, *From the river to the sea, Palestine will be free!* A survey in the field showed that many of the students did not know which river and sea this entailed, but everyone knew what the words "Let's kill the Jews" meant. Nobody was shouting, "Two states for two peoples!" Thus, the call for genocide was heard around the world.

The complacency stemming from hard-won modern achievements, our scientific preeminence in the world, the promise of the Abraham Accords, the idea of belonging to a democracy surrounded by enemies calling for its destruction, the ambition to be a country equal to others, one that survives internal quarrels and rifts — all of this is an essential component of Israeli society. Israel, like the rest of the West, is egalitarian, ecological, global, technologically advanced, and very modern, full of young people who tell you proudly how deeply they are involved in high-tech and startups, who glory in protesting against perceived injustice or mistaken policy, such as the Supreme Court reform, even to the point of not showing up for reserve duty. But when disaster struck, all Israelis came running to defend their home with brilliant patriotic spirit.

Looking through its theocratic window, Hamas had witnessed Israeli pilots, the flower of Israel, risk undermining the army with their political protest and call for conscientious military objection, while the ruling right-wing railed against them. Both sides were wrong: both needed to renounce their goals as the collective hatred toward Israel emerged; antisemitism took center stage like an enormous, macroscopic, dangerous puppet while Israel bled. A long-standing ideological trend that started in the Soviet Union and later evolved into Third-Worldism has now merged with Islamism. This trend originally intended to support impoverished countries but ended up harming them, often leading to increased poverty and instability. Combined with radical Islamism, Third-Worldism has created a potent mix that fuels anti-Western sentiments and justifies terrorism. Together, they form a narrative that portrays Western nations, especially the U.S. and its allies (including Israel), as oppressors, and thus justifying extreme measures in the name of resistance. Those "isms" (Third-Worldism and Islamism) have destroyed all attempts at peace, and led the Palestinians to reject every offer of coexistence. But the world keeps trying, and even Biden, ignoring the fact that the Palestinians of the Palestinian Authority are all ideologically pro-Hamas, again offers the two-state formula that has already failed and led to catastrophes.

What Hamas did to the inhabitants of Kibbutz Be'eri is the final and definitive confirmation, leaving no alternatives for Israel but war or surrender. While I sat waiting to watch the 47-minute Hamas atrocity film, I wanted to understand how far antisemitism can go, to fathom the hatred of a human being for a newborn baby only because he is Jewish. Like a child on the Tel Aviv beach, I saw the tsunami wave of hate rising as high as a mountain, and I could not escape. I am a child in the face of the history of antisemitism, against which the only victory was the State of Israel, and now the walls of this citadel are again being besieged.

However, Hamas outstrips Hitler's Nazis and Schutzstaffel (the SS), whose propaganda about exterminating the Jews was less explicit; the decision was mentioned only in Germany and in Italy, without a display of trophies or an overt flaunting of triumph in the world. Here, however, one of the novelties is the absolute and unvarnished exhibition of the most virulent racist hatred that exists: radical antisemitism. Hamas and its supporters not only display it, they are proud of it.

While they were teaching the people to hate the Jews, the Nazis did not flaunt the unprecedented violence that was taking place, did not publicize photographs of gas chambers or of mothers with their children in their arms on the edge of the mass grave into which they would fall after a blast of Nazi guns. The Nazis got drunk at night, Douglas Murray recounts, because the commanders consoled them with alcohol for what they had done. Here, however, the young terrorists from Gaza filmed themselves laughing, riding motorcycles, driving pickup trucks, raping and disemboweling women and then shooting them in the head. All for public display.

For Hamas, the goal of the extermination of the Jews is a cosmic quest. Allah will be pleased, and the day will come when Islam will rule the world. This belief accompanied the brutal and primitive executions and mass rape.

Hamas's aim, like that of ISIS and Al Qaeda, is to terrorize. This Islamist goal stems from an ecstatic interpretation of a religion, and it is critical to acknowledge that not all interpretations include that. But nobody can explain how it is possible to decide to cut off the arm of an eight-year-old girl and to let her shiver for hours, bathed in her own blood, until she dies, if it is not motivated by a maniacal, transcendental ambition. Nobody can explain how it is possible to kill a mother and father in front of their three-year-old child, and then abduct her alone in a vehicle to Gaza. Yet all this happened. Nor can one explain how it is possible to slaughter a group of little girls all sitting together in hiding, holding each other's hands to gain courage. Yet this also happened. We are here to try and will bear witness to it forever because denialism, whether of the Holocaust or of the events of October 7, is the most classic form of rehabilitation of the monsters and the basis, even today, of the fiercest antisemitism. When naysayers deny the existence of these horrific events, it isn't just distorting the truth — it is essentially excusing, even justifying, the actions of those who committed the atrocities. This kind of denial is dangerous because it allows the same hateful ideologies to persist and even thrive. By refusing to acknowledge the reality of these events, deniers undermine the victims' suffering and give a free pass to the perpetrators, extending the cycle of hatred and violence.

The wave of antisemitism against the dead and the live Jews came unexpectedly. It is also no longer true that many people "love dead Jews" and not living Jews. They do not like any of them. Twelve hundred heinous deaths were not enough. The denialism erupted immediately after the world's most public massacre. In the name of the UN, Secretary-General Guterres insisted that the background to the violence was the guilt of the Jews, a claim that the world has repeated throughout history and that has flourished since the Jews gained a country and an army.

Gaza fell into Israeli hands after a war of defense, not because of a decision to take that cursed piece of land, which Cairo, which also shares a border with it, had never wanted.

Even the antisemites on the campuses hold only misconceptions. It is false that Israel occupied the "Palestinian state," which has never existed. The idea that the Jews originally had no connection with the land of Israel is false: anybody who has read even a little history knows that Israel is the land of the Jewish people and that Jerusalem is its lifeblood. This is the country in which the Jews have their roots. This is proven though biblical geography and the great love that is as alive as ever. It is upon Jerusalem that the entire morality of the monotheistic and civilized world rests.

Today, the Hamas murderers enjoy the support of bastions of culture, those that formulated the "religion" of our times — human rights. And yet, this religion is now in danger of shattering because of the double standard that cannot see Russia, China, and Iran's flagrant violation of those human rights. To the shame of the world, Iran even holds the presidency of the UN Human Rights Commission. An appeal like the one that 4,000 academics in Italy signed, demanding the cessation of cooperation with Israeli universities after October 7, will forever stand out in the history of ignorance and ignominy. The refusal of the feminist organizations to recognize Israeli women's irremediable pain after multiple rapes and the accompanying scars, fractures, wounds, and murders, used serially as weapons of collective terrorism and domination, will remain on the conscience of the United Nations forever, even if it eventually recorded a weak condemnation.

The reaction of the "woke square," the cultural and academic institutions and their various associations, has shown how the uncritical and ignorants' embrace of Third-Worldism is deep-rooted and dangerous for the very civilization in which we live. The cultural background of the new antisemitism, which some Jews share, is constructed on the latest "sophisticated" lie that has transformed the Jewish people into a mass of "oppressors" determined to "dominate," "occupy," " exploit" and commit "genocide." Based on this determination (which the European Union endorsed after intentionally misinterpreting the 1967 resolutions that envisage a solution that the Palestinians have consistently rejected), Hamas exterminated the most significant number of Jews in one single day since the Holocaust, and kidnapped 240 of them, including infants and the elderly.

In a fictional Palestine — that entity "from the river to the sea," which, having never existed, can be imagined at will, according to the most perfect antisemitic dream — all the Jews are annihilated. Twelve hundred fatalities in a small country like Israel correspond to 50,000 citizens in the United States, and the hostages, again comparatively, to about 5,000 people. Nobody can imagine that the United States or any European country would agree to be "humanitarian" like Israel, which, instead of carpet-bombing all of the terrorist murderers in one day, has adopted a strategy that allows the Gaza civilians to evacuate the war zone. No leaders, knowing that the war criminal Yahya Sinwar could be hiding under a hospital building, would order their soldiers to enter on tiptoe rather than bombing the building. Yet, Israel has tried to bring medicines, incubators, and food for the medical staff and the sick, and to evacuate patients wherever possible.

Today's antisemitic allegations against Israel are neither more nor less than the ancient accusations of deicide, the blood libel that gave ideological sanction to antisemitism at the time of the Holocaust and long before. It is of no importance to the accusers that Hamas kills gays, that in Gaza parents give their little girls in marriage to adult pedophiles, and that Gazan men oppress women using beatings, polygamy, and segregation. Over the years, I have seen cartoons in which Ariel Sharon eats Palestinian children with his chest covered with their blood, and I have heard a French ambassador call Israel "that shitty little country" after the suicide bombers blew up buses carrying children on the way to school and old people in slippers. Standing history on its head, people call the Jews colonizers and the Palestinians colonized, the Jews aggressors and the Palestinians aggressed, the Jews warmongers and the Palestinians pacifists. I have seen the denial of every historical truth and have not missed the spectacle of the Western mobs bellowing in approval of every act of cruelty toward the citizens of Israel. I have seen newspapers condemning Israel because the "Al-Aqsa Mosque was in danger!" Hamas's war cry. Yet, when Hamas targeted Jerusalem in 2021 with rockets, it seemed that Al-Aqsa was worth far less to them than the chance of hitting the homes of the Jews.

For those in Israel, there is a great consolation: On the day of the massacre, from every corner of the country, men and women rushed to help in staggering numbers and with astounding altruism. A resident of Be'eri, one of the kibbutzim that Hamas razed, was on the beach in Tel Aviv sunbathing. He reached the kibbutz, frantic, two and a half hours later, even though it was forbidden to travel on highways still infested with terrorists carrying out their massacres. He headed a group of heroes who joined together by chance and ventured into the now-incinerated streets of Be'eri, where, trying to free the people barricaded in the dining hall, they met their deaths. I talked with dozens of youngsters who grabbed whatever they could find — a knife, a stick — in the face of the invaders' machine guns and came out of besieged homes to defend their mothers and siblings from the terrorists. A father who, from hundreds of kilometers away, rushed like a madman to the kibbutz where his daughter lived and snatched her from death, managing to push her out the back window of the house where she had been under siege. A mother who, while terrorists were shooting and torturing, followed her son everywhere, collecting the wounded, as he ventured into the kibbutz trying to save whomever he could; when her son was shot, she drove him home and returned to rescue other boys. An older woman kept a gang of terrorists at bay in her home by feeding them, saving the whole family with her composure until help arrived. I interviewed a man who, with one leg severed from his body, held out for about ten hours, shielding his family until he saw his son and wife die, riddled with bullets; almost completely drained of blood, he resisted, determined to at least save his daughter. On the day of the attack, police officers and soldiers entered Gaza to fight and gave their lives there.

In the war, the episodes of heroism multiplied: Twenty-five-year-old Gal and nineteen-year-old Mahor Cohen, the son and nephew of former chief of staff Gadi Eisenkot, now a member of the war cabinet, were killed in battle. Wracked with grief, Eisenkot expressed how honored he felt to have been the father and the uncle of two young soldiers; the following day, he was back at work. Israel's president, Isaac Herzog, waited for word from his son, who was fighting in Gaza, because the use of telephones from the field is forbidden. All of Israel has sons, daughters, grandchildren, spouses, and parents forced into a war of defense against the terrorists who decapitated babies. On October 7, 360,000 reserve soldiers rushed to save the country. Many thousands of Israelis working or touring overseas rushed to airports to fly home, even sitting in the aisles and washrooms of El Al planes. They appeared at their reserve units, demanding equipment and orders without call-up papers. Since then, they have been fighting, some to their last breath, and will continue to do so until they achieve the victory that is indispensable for Israel's security.

Israel is a country of heroes. At the Nova Festival, the young people who had been dancing tried to protect each other at the cost of their lives. Desperate girls tried to save their friends from rape, torture, and murder, and fell victim to this themselves. By the hundreds, soldiers sacrificed themselves; not yet dressed, they jumped out of the besieged barracks and fought against the surprise attack with bare hands. Without knowing what they would find, the police officers threw themselves into battle despite the astounding numbers of terrorists. The women soldiers who, at their observation posts, had seen and warned of the black tide that was rushing toward Israel, stayed at their screens even after realizing that nobody wanted to believe the truth. They were alone and they gave their lives. Visit the reserve soldiers at the front today — secular and religious, Ashkenazi and Sephardi — who have been sleeping in the mud and eating cans of tuna since October 7. You will discover, in the aftermath of Israel's political imbroglio, the message of unity and complete dedication to defending their country. By comparison, in Europe and the United States, personal interest and convenience overcome national spirit.

Israel is the unrecognized experiment of what a democratic state can be when faced with a challenge and genuine danger. It offers a picture of what young people can become when they have faith and a common purpose, when they acknowledge their duties in addition to their rights. Even those born with the proverbial silver spoons in their mouths recognize that they can die in battle.

What has changed since October 7 is that now we know that terrorism can morph from an ambush into a global strategic threat, first by killing unsuspecting civilians, police officers, and soldiers and then endangering Jewish communities worldwide. The terrorists call on world powers, primarily Iran and Russia, for support for their aggressions in the Middle East and the West.

Therefore, let us hope for victory over evil, a triumph of what we love and believe in. Let us hope for democracy and common sense, that will prevail not with a premature ceasefire, but only when evil is stamped out.

The Silent Suffering: Revealing Hamas's Brutality and Global Silence

Moshe Kaplan, MD
based on articles written by Yvette Alt Miller on Aish.com

If anyone had any doubt about the atrocities of October 7, this essay by Yvette Alt Miller presents some of the horrifying details. Our review confirms that multiple sources substantiate her compelling piece.

On October 7th, 2023, the world was horrified by the sheer scale of violence that Hamas unleashed on Israeli civilians. The aftermath of the attack revealed horrifying details of physical, sexual, and emotional abuse inflicted not only during the initial assault but also throughout the captivity of hostages. Despite the clear evidence, recognition of these atrocities has been disturbingly slow, and biased narratives and outright denials have marred the global community's response.

One of the most harrowing testimonies comes from Nili Margalit, who was abducted by Palestinian civilians and sold to Hamas. Margalit recounted her ordeal of being dragged from her burning home, driven to the Gaza border, and taken into a tunnel where she was held captive. Her experience reflects the systematic brutality and the complicity of local civilians in these heinous acts. This transactional violence highlights the deeply ingrained hatred and dehumanization that fuels such atrocities.

The terror extended beyond physical violence to include severe sexual abuse. In late March 2024, Amit Soussana, a 40-year-old freed hostage, became the first to speak publicly about having been sexually assaulted. She detailed how she was chained in darkness, forced to commit sexual acts on her Hamas guard — known as Muhammad — who repeatedly assailed her at gunpoint. Soussana's harrowing account underscores the pervasive sexual violence that many hostages endured. The reports of medical professionals, including senior Israeli gynecologist Dr. Julia Barda and social worker Valeria Tsekhovsky, corroborate her story, providing undeniable proof of the abuse.

The brutality was not limited to women. Both male and female hostages faced extreme violence and sexual abuse. Maya Regev, who was severely injured and kidnapped from the Nova Music Festival, testified that all female captives were subjected to sexual harassment. Regev's brother, Itai, endured a botched surgery without anesthesia while in captivity. The siblings' experiences reflect the indiscriminate cruelty that the hostages faced, further highlighting the depravity of their captors.

One of the most shocking revelations came from Israeli police investigations. Chief Superintendent Yaron Binyamin disclosed that Hamas terrorists mutilated their victims, taking body parts back to Gaza to use as leverage in future negotiations. The testimonies of captured terrorists have confirmed this grotesque practice; in their reports, they showed no remorse for their actions. Binyamin's statement emphasizes the methodical and sadistic nature of Hamas's violence.

Survivors of the October 7th attacks also reported witnessing extreme acts of sexual violence. Raz Cohen, Nova survivor, described seeing terrorists laughing as they raped and murdered a woman. The attackers treated the violence as entertainment, further dehumanizing their victims. This casual brutality, combined with the systemic nature of the abuse, paints a chilling picture of the environment that Hamas created.

The global response to these atrocities has been disappointingly muted. It took until December for the UN Women's agency to condemn Hamas's gender-based violence. Israeli feminist organizations and public figures have criticized this delay, and the general silence of global feminist organizations, especially given the severity of the crimes. The lack of immediate recognition and response has further traumatized the victims and their families, who struggle to find justice for and acknowledgment of their suffering.

The fact that some segments of the international community deny these atrocities exacerbates the issue. Basem Naim, a spokesperson for Hamas, dismissed Soussana's testimony as potentially fabricated. Such disavowals, despite overwhelming evidence, hinder efforts to hold perpetrators accountable and provide justice for the victims. This denialism also reflects the broader issue of biased narratives that seek to downplay or deny the suffering of Israeli victims.

The detailed accounts of the physical, sexual, and emotional abuse that Hamas has inflicted since October 7th present a clear and harrowing picture of their brutality.

These stories underscore the urgent need for the international community to recognize and condemn these atrocities unequivocally. The survivors' courage in sharing their experiences should serve as a powerful reminder of the horrors they endured and the need for justice and accountability.

A UN report in March 2024 concluded there was "clear and convincing information" that Israeli hostages in Gaza experienced "sexual violence, including rape." The report also found "reasonable grounds" to believe such abuse was ongoing. This report, while not investigative in nature, aimed to collect and confirm allegations, noting that a "fully fledged" investigation would be needed to establish definitive proof.

The attacks on Israeli communities, in which 1,139 people were killed and 240 hostages were kidnapped and taken to Gaza, involved widespread sexual violence. The Israel Defense Forces and Israeli officials have provided evidence suggesting that Hamas terrorists raped, sexually abused, and mutilated hundreds of Israeli women. Hamas fighters infiltrated Israeli towns, where witnesses reported that they tortured, raped, and sexually assaulted many women, girls, and some men.

For example, a paramedic from the 669 Special Tactics Rescue Unit at Kibbutz Be'eri found the bodies of two teenage girls in a bedroom, one of whom had been raped. Other accounts from survivors and first responders detailed instances of gang rape, mutilation, and severe physical abuse. Tel Aviv University professor Tamar Herzig reported that militants discussed plans to rape specific girls and paraded victims with their clothes ripped off and blood between their legs.

Hamas has denied committing these atrocities, citing

Islamic teachings that forbid such acts. However, numerous reports and testimonies contradict these denials. Israeli security agencies collected extensive evidence, including video footage and photographs of victims' bodies, confirming the accounts of sexual assault. Autopsies of victims corroborated these reports, revealing signs of rape, genital mutilation, and severe trauma. This denial hinders efforts to hold perpetrators accountable and provide justice for the victims.

The silence and slow response of global organizations, coupled with biased narratives that downplay or deny the suffering of Israeli victims, only add to the victims' trauma. It is imperative that the world hear their voices and acknowledge their stories in order to ensure that such horrors are never repeated. The world must stand with the victims, condemn the perpetrators, and work tirelessly to bring justice to those who have suffered at the hands of Hamas.

In February 2024, the Association of Rape Crisis Centers in Israel (ARCCI) published a comprehensive 35-page report detailing the extent of the sexual violence during the October 7th attacks. The findings, partly based on statements from ZAKA members, revealed that these assaults were widespread. The ARCCI document highlighted that Hamas members often deliberately carried out the rapes in the presence of an audience, including partners, family members, or friends, amplifying the pain, humiliation, and trauma for all involved. It concluded that there was clear evidence of "systematic, targeted sexual abuse" of women during the Hamas-led assault on southern Israel.

Adding to this, in December 2023, *The New York Times* published an investigative report, entitled *Screams*

Without Words: How Hamas Weaponized Sexual Violence on Oct. 7, which provided a detailed account of the rape and sexual violence during the attack. The article described how Hamas systematically used sexual violence as a weapon of war. Despite facing criticism for relying heavily on witness testimony and lacking some forensic evidence, *The Times* stood by its report, asserting that it was rigorously sourced and edited. Recently, World Israel News disclosed the discovery of vocabulary lists — Hebrew words transliterated into Arabic — so that the terrorists could command their captives "don't talk," "take off your clothes," and "spread your legs," among other phrases. The infiltrators also carried notes reminding them to "show no mercy," and to mutilate their captives' bodies.

The UN also took a significant step in addressing these crimes. In early March 2024, UN Special Representative on Sexual Violence in Conflict, Pramila Patten, brought a United Nations team to Israel to investigate Hamas's acts of rape. During the week-long visit, Patten and her team reviewed raw footage from October 7th, met with released captives from Gaza, and heard their testimonies. Patten visited various locations, including the Nova Festival site in Re'im, Gaza border communities, and the military base in Nahal Oz, to gain insights into Hamas's sexual crimes.

Upon her return, Patten released a report concluding that there were "reasonable grounds to believe that conflict-related sexual violence occurred during the October 7th attacks." The report detailed instances of rape and gang rape in multiple locations, including the Nova Music Festival, Road 232, and Kibbutz Re'im. The UN report further noted credible circumstantial evidence indicating genital mutilation, sexualized torture, and other forms of cruel, inhuman, and degrading treatment. It also highlighted "clear and convincing information" that Israeli hostages in Gaza were subjected to sexual violence, including rape and sexualized torture. Although the UN team couldn't independently verify every media report of sexual violence due to the lack of a fully fledged investigation, it confirmed that the information that Israeli national institutions provided was authentic and unmanipulated. Patten's submitted her team's findings to the UN Secretary-General and the Security Council, emphasizing the need for accountability.

Meanwhile, Hamas officials, including Basem Naim, continue to deny the use of sexual violence as a weapon of war, citing Islamic principles that forbid any sexual relationship outside of marriage. Hamas accused Western media of bias and said the reports of sexual violence demonized Palestinian resistance. They demanded that *The New York Times* apologize for publishing its report and blamed any sexual violence that occurred on other militants who joined Hamas in the breaching of the Israel-Gaza border on October 7th.

Despite the overwhelming evidence, some international responses have been inadequate. The UN, particularly the Committee on the Elimination of Discrimination Against Women (CEDAW), did not condemn the rapes of Israeli women, even after receiving evidence and witness testimonies. Israeli First Lady Michal Herzog called the lack of response an "inconceivable and unforgivable silence." UN Women briefly condemned Hamas in a post but deleted it shortly thereafter, highlighting its inconsistent and tepid reaction to these atrocities.

On November 28th, UN Secretary-General António Guterres acknowledged the numerous accounts of sexual violence during the October 7th attack, stating that these incidents "must be vigorously investigated and prosecuted." A UN commission of inquiry investigating war crimes on both sides of the Israel-Hamas conflict will include a focus on instances of Hamas's use of sexual violence.

The unrelenting brutality of Hamas and the international community's slow, often inadequate, response highlight the urgent need for a unified and unequivocal condemnation of these crimes. The traumatic personal experiences that survivors like Soussana and Regev have bravely shared underscore the critical importance of recognizing and addressing Hamas's atrocities. Their testimonies, along with the corroborating evidence that Israeli security agencies and international investigators have collected, provide a stark and undeniable account of Hamas's systematic and targeted sexual violence.

The chilling confessions of terrorists, and the testimonies of survivors, reveal the depth of cruelty and dehumanization that characterized the attacks on October 7th and the subsequent captivity of the hostages. Hamas's systematic use of sexual violence as a weapon of war is a clear violation of human rights and international law. The stories of Nili Margalit, Chen Goldstein-Almog, and countless others who endured unimaginable horrors serve as a powerful call to action for the global community.

It is imperative that the world hear the voices of the victims and acknowledge their stories. The international community must stand in solidarity with the survivors, demand accountability for the perpetrators, and ensure that justice is served. The international community must work to prevent such atrocities from occurring again and to support the survivors as they rebuild their lives in the aftermath of such traumatic experiences. We must never forget the horrors that Hamas inflicted on October 7th, 2023, and the global community must remain vigilant in its efforts to uphold justice and human dignity.

Why the World Loves Hamas and Hates Israel

Noa Tishby

Here we present Noa Tishby's Youtube video expressing her views on why the world loves Hamas and hates Israel. It offers a clear and compelling discussion of the subject, which will clear up some misconceptions for anyone seeking the truth.

ISRAEL IS IN a precarious situation today, surrounded by enemies with genocidal intentions. These groups openly declare their aim to destroy Israel and kill its people. It's crucial to take these threats seriously because those enemies are not hiding their intentions. This dire situation is made worse by support from sympathizers in the West, many of whom may not even realize the full implications of their actions.

Over the past decade, there has been a massive effort, costing about $1 trillion, to sway American youth against Israel. This campaign has been waged through various channels, including PR campaigns from Al Jazeera, ethnic studies programs in high schools, the Boycott, Divestment, and Sanctions (BDS) movement, and groups like Students for Justice in Palestine (SJP) on college campuses. The result? Many young Americans, including Jews, have been indoctrinated to oppose Israel, often without the Jewish community fully noticing or addressing the problem.

Imagine if a war led to the massacre of one million Jews. The indoctrinated masses in the West, who have been taught to see Jews as colonizers, might actually justify or accept such an atrocity. This isn't a new reality, but awareness of it is growing, and it's time to notice and push back.

On college campuses, Jewish students are being ostracized, marginalized, and demonized. They're being pushed out of social circles, and this issue hasn't been taken seriously enough. A decade ago in Los Angeles, Israel was already being thrown under the bus, with an obsessive focus on that country, unlike any other nation. Among progressives and elites, the conversation has shifted from criticizing specific Israeli policies to questioning Israel's very right to exist, labeling it a colonialist endeavor. This shift has unleashed open antisemitism, almost as if a long-simmering abscess has burst.

Elites who claim to be saving the world are actually targeting the smallest minority: the Jews. Their actions aren't about social justice; they're part of an antisemitic agenda aimed at destroying Israel.

Many Jews in America have sought acceptance and likability, which has led some to become anti-Israel. They mistakenly believe that by distancing themselves from Israel, they're saving themselves or being accepted by the "cool" crowd. History has repeatedly shown how wrong this belief is.

It's heartbreaking to see these individuals delude themselves into thinking they are "good Jews" by separating themselves from Israel. No matter what the Israeli government does, it wouldn't change their minds — they're just making excuses. Yet, despite all these challenges, the very existence of the Jewish people remains one of the greatest miracles in history.

The horrors of genocidal rape and multiple perpetrator rape (MPR) provide valuable insights into the current situation Israel faces. Just as genocidal rape is a deliberate strategy to annihilate communities, the genocidal intentions of Israel's enemies are a calculated effort to destroy the Jewish state. Recognizing these intentions as genuine threats, rather than mere rhetoric, is crucial for developing appropriate defensive strategies.

The propaganda employed by groups like Hamas and the influence of anti-Israel movements in the West represent a form of psychological warfare aimed at weakening Israel's support base and isolating it globally. This mirrors the use of psychological tactics in wartime sexual violence to demoralize and destroy the fabric of communities.

Group dynamics play a significant role in both MPR and anti-Israel activism. Just as MPR involves group cohesion and peer pressure to commit atrocities, anti-Israel activists on campuses and in the media utilize groupthink and social influence to foster antisemitic sentiments. Understanding these dynamics can help in crafting effective counter-strategies.

The long-term impact of sustained anti-Israel propaganda has created a stigma around supporting Israel, one similar to the social stigma faced by survivors of genocidal rape. Addressing and reversing these stigmas requires a concerted effort to educate and change perceptions, much like supporting and healing for victims of wartime sexual violence.

While Israel's enemies employ manipulation and violence, Israel's actions are guided by a strong moral compass and a commitment to humanitarian principles. By understanding the true nature of Hamas and its supporters, and by recognizing Israel's efforts to uphold ethical standards even in the face of adversity, we gain a clearer perspective on the conflict. The path to peace is fraught with challenges, but Israel's dedication to truth, responsibility, and humanity provides a beacon of hope for a just and lasting resolution.

No Peace with Terror: International Community Must Support a Hamas-Free Future

Ari H. Orkaby

T̲ʜᴇ ɢʀᴏᴛᴇsǫᴜᴇ sᴘᴇᴄᴛᴀᴄʟᴇ on 19 January of three female hostages, tortured for 470 days in Gaza's jails, being paraded through a hostile crowd before their release to the Red Cross, encapsulates the barbarism of Hamas.

This tragic event underscores the reality that Hamas bears full responsibility for the war that broke on that day and subsequently brought about the suffering inflicted on both Israelis and Palestinians and the devastation of Gaza.

The time has come for the global community to confront this truth: there's no hope with Hamas. There's no peace with Hamas. Hamas is a roadblock to peace and stability, and its continued rule over Gaza spells ruin for the Palestinians and for the region.

Hamas's boundless brutality was laid bare on October 7, when its forces launched an unprecedented attack on Israel, bombing cities and villages, burning homes on their inhabitants, raping and maiming, killing over 1,400 civilians, as well as taking more than 250 hostages, including children, babies and the elderly.

Countless families shattered by violence

These actions shattered countless families in a wave of violence that continues to haunt the region. Yet, the suffering does not stop with Israelis.

Gazans, too, bear the brunt of Hamas's destructive governance. While claiming to champion Palestinian liberation, Hamas has prioritized dictatorship and militarization over the well-being of its people, instrumentalizing humanitarian aid as a means of oppression and redirecting resources toward building tunnels and stockpiling weapons.

The humanitarian crisis in Gaza is a direct consequence of Hamas's misrule, which reduced Gaza to a landscape of despair. Not only now but also before the October 7 attack, Gaza's basic infrastructure lies in ruins, the economy was in a wreck, healthcare was inadequate, and unemployment soared, exceeding 50% (World Bank, 2023).

Hamas's obsession with armed conflict has trapped Gazans in perpetual suffering, with no vision for a future beyond war. The most blatant illustration is the construction of hundreds of kilometers of terror tunnels, which Hamas used to smuggle arms and also imprison and torture Israeli hostages. Still, they deny entry to Gazan citizens for shelter.

Hamas's obsession with armed conflict has trapped Gazans in perpetual suffering. Beyond the tangible destruction, Hamas's Nazi ideology fosters a culture of martyrdom and hatred, perpetuating cycles of violence. The education system in Gaza, under Hamas's control, glorifies violence and jihad over coexistence and peace, as reported by the Institute for Monitoring Peace and Cultural Tolerance in School Education Institute (IMPACT-se, 2023).

Hamas's stranglehold on Gaza forecloses any hope for a better future. For Gazans, this means living under a regime that prioritizes violence over prosperity. For Israelis, it means enduring relentless attacks that upend lives and undermine the hope for peace.

And for the broader region, Hamas represents a destabilizing force that perpetuates cycles of hostility and promotes radical Islamism and Iranian interests. Indeed, Hamas's allegiance to Iran—the so-called "axis of evil"—further entangles the region in turmoil, as Tehran's influence fuels extremism and aggression.

The international community must be vocal and recognize that a Gaza ruled by Hamas offers no pathway to peace, only a continuation of conflict, suffering, and instability for both the Palestinians and Israelis.

The removal of Hamas is not merely an Israeli interest; it is a regional necessity. Without Hamas, Gaza could rebuild. Without Hamas, Gazans and Israelis might begin to envision a future unshackled from perpetual conflict.

A few hours ago, it was reported that, in a meeting with the Egyptian intelligence chief, an agreement was reached with the heads of the Mossad and Shin Bet that the Palestinian Authority will manage the Rafah Crossing under international supervision and monitoring by the UN.

The Prime Minister's Office confirmed the involvement of the Palestinian Authority at the Rafah Crossing, alongside Gazans "who are not affiliated with Hamas and have been vetted by the Shin Bet."

This is a good start, but it is imperative that the global community acts decisively and supports efforts to dismantle Hamas's power structure.

Hamas's continued rule guarantees only despair for Gazans, perpetual fear for Israelis, and enduring instability for the region. The world must not stand idly by. Now is the time to envision and work toward a future where the shadow of Hamas no longer looms over the Middle East.

The Most Evil Society in Human History

Gary Willig

What would the most evil society ever created by humans be like?

Such a society would outwardly display its depravity by elevating the most evil man in history to sainthood, perhaps by naming stores "Hitler" and making Mein Kampf a best-seller.

Such a society would teach its children not to love life, but to love death, not to seek to make the world a better place, but that their only goal in life should be to wipe out an entire ethnicity.

Such a society would welcome and cheer the deaths of tens of thousands of their own people if it meant they could kill a fraction of that number of innocents in a murderous frenzy.

A society where death is the highest value, where genocide is the only goal to work towards, and where goodness itself is not allowed to exist. There could be nothing more evil than that.

The murder of Shir, Ariel, and Kfir Bibas is just the latest proof that Gaza under Hamas is exactly such a society, the most evil society in human history.

It was hardly a surprise when it was confirmed last week that the youngest hostages were killed. We hoped against hope that Hamas would put practicality and the fact that these innocent children were more valuable alive than dead above their bloodlust, even knowing that the October 7th massacre already proved that Hamas' bloodlust outweighs its common sense by orders of magnitude.

But the depth of the evil is still shocking. In the early days of the war, when Hamas was negotiating the first ceasefire of November 2023, the monsters who held the Bibas family captive could not restrain themselves for even two months and murdered a baby and a toddler before they could be released.

They strangled a four-year-old boy and a ten-month-old baby with their bare hands. Who does that? Who could possibly be that evil as to use their bare hands to kill a baby who is not even old enough to start walking or talking?

At every turn, Hamas has demonstrated its depravity. It wrote on the supposed coffin of Shiri Bibas that she was "arrested" when she was kidnapped from her home with her two small children for the "crime" of being born Jewish, the same crime that earned Ariel and Kfir the death sentence of the jihadists. It then returned the wrong body, continuing to hold Shiri's body like a sick trophy. The keys it provided to unlock the coffins did not work, deliberately adding further insult to injury. And it mutilated the bodies of those beautiful children in a pathetic attempt to cover up its crimes and blame Israel for what it did.

Kfir will never learn to walk or talk. He will never learn to sing the ABCs or the Aleph-Bet or even Baby Shark. He'll never discover Elmo or Barney or Peppa Pig. He'll never go to preschool. And all because a group of evil people think that Jewish babies like him do not deserve to live.

Hitler is deified in Gaza, where a store became wildly successful thanks to being given the name "Hitler 2" by its Nazi-worshiping owner. In Hamastan, Hitler is in Gaza a prophet of a far greater level than Mohammed, Mein Kampf is a thousand times holier than the Koran, and death is their true god, to whom even Allah is but a mere servant.

This evil is so widespread in Gaza that not a single person out of more than two million made a single attempt to help or free a single hostage. Unlike Europe in the 1940s, there were no righteous among the nations in Gaza. Not even the promise of five million dollars could compel a single Gazan to treat a single Jew as anything other than someone to be killed.

The cause of Jihad is only different from the cause of Nazism in that it seeks Islamist supremacy rather than Aryan supremacy, but otherwise the two are nearly identical. Both seek to take over the entire world and impose a permanent global dictatorship. Both are inherently genocidal and seek the annihilation of the entire Jewish people wherever they are as well as all who others do not fit their narrow view of the "elect."

Israelis are far too used to this evil. In 1979, PLO terrorist Samir Kuntar invaded Nahariya from Lebanon and crushed the skull of four-year-old Einat Haran against a rock with a rifle, an attack which also resulted in the death of Einat's two-year-old sister Yael. In 2001, a sniper deliberately shot 10-month-old Shalhevet Pass, the exact same age as Kfir Bibas when he was murdered, in the head while she sat in her stroller. In 2011, terrorists murdered five members of the Fogel family in their beds, stabbing parents Ehud and Ruth, 11-year-old Yoav, four-year-old Elad, and newborn Hadas. Those animals stabbed a 3-month-old baby to death in her crib.

Those are just a handful of the far too many times beasts in human form killed babies and toddlers for the crime of being born Jews.

The death-loving evil of Hamas is not new. It originated with Hitler and his pal, the Mufti of Jerusalem, who loved the concentration and death camps the Nazis built to slaughter Jews far more than he was capable of loving another living being. Yasser Arafat and his joke of a successor, Mahmoud Abbas, embodied the same evil and taught their people to worship death instead of Allah and seek to murder and destroy rather than to build and create.

The global response to the worst evil imaginable has been disgusting. The more Jewish children, the more Jewish babies, that are murdered, the more global support for the baby-killers and would-be genociders grows. Marches in support of Hamas began on October 7th not in spite of the massacre committed that day, but because of the largest massacre of Jews since the Holocaust.

Those who gather on college campuses like Columbia, on the streets of New York, London, and Sydney, do not support Hamas because they think there should be a Palestinian Arab state. They support Hamas because it kills babies. Those who shout the loudest about a nonexistent "genocide" want nothing more than to see a real genocide. They are exactly the same as people marching in support of Nazi Germany in 1945. They knowingly embrace evil and are evil themselves.

This includes the United Nations and its representatives like Francesca Albanese, who never once tweeted about the Bibas children and who spent the day their bodies were returned trying to shore up support for Hamas in Spain. It includes so-called human rights NGOs like Amnesty International and the Red Cross, which knowingly and deliberately abandoned the innocent Jewish hostages to torture and death, just as the Red Cross abandoned millions of Jews to death during the Holocaust. They have decreed from on high that Jews do not have the right to live and Hamas has the right to take children hostage and murder them at its leisure.

Evil of this nature and magnitude cannot be tolerated and cannot be allowed to continue to fester. It can only be fought and destroyed. When a society worships death as its god, when it is geared towards nothing but committing genocide against another people, when it raises children to do nothing but murder the children of others, that society must be defeated once and for all, just as the Nazis and Imperial Japan were defeated 80 years ago. Only when they are forced to give up their hate, their love of death and murder, as the Germans were forced to do when Hitler died, can the people who remain in Gaza have any kind of future. Only when evil is purged from Gaza can there be any hope of anything other than the death Hamas worships and loves so dearly.

To allow Hamas to endure, to allow Jihadism, Islamism, and genocidal antisemitism to endure, guarantees more hate, more death, more destruction, more murdered men, women, and children, and yes, more murders of babies.

End Hamas. End the dreams of its fellow death-lovers in the Ivy Leagues and the halls of the UN of another Holocaust. End the killings of Jewish babies. End the most evil society humanity has ever seen.

Charles Manson and the Bibas Victims of Hamas

Rabbi Yair Hoffman

THE RELEASE OF the holy bodies of the Bibas family Hashem brings back childhood memories. Directly behind my home when I was growing up was an empty reservoir. Behind that reservoir was something called the Spahn Ranch. This was the ranch that housed the depraved Manson Family, led by Charles Manson.

Back then, kids were not so sheltered—we were exposed to it all. We all watched the news together as the horrors unfolded.

Some moments leave an indelible scar on the soul, not only for their depraved brutality but for what they reveal about the terrifying depths of human cruelty. The Manson Family murders and the October 7th, 2023, attack in Israel are two such events—separated by over half a century but bound by the same horrifying threads of depravity and the calculated targeting of the innocent. These were not random acts of violence. They were meticulously crafted nightmares, orchestrated by monsters.

Charles Manson was not just a killer—he was a master manipulator who turned human beings into executioners. He preyed upon the vulnerable, drawing in followers with a lethal blend of psychological control—no different from Hamas and the residents of Gaza. His ultimate goal was not just destruction—it was terror, a primal, gut-wrenching fear that would shatter American society.

The nights of the Manson murders brought that terror to life. Sharon Tate—eight months pregnant, filled with the promise of new life—was slaughtered along with her friends in a frenzied bloodbath. The murderers carved messages in blood, their depravity on full display. Later, Leno and Rosemary LaBianca were subjected to a similar fate, murdered with that same cold-blooded evil cruelty.

Fast forward to October 7, 2023. "He sits in ambush in the villages; in hiding places he murders the innocent" (Psalms 10:8-9). Hamas murderers launched their depraved coordinated attack on Israeli communities, massacring over 1,200 innocent people in a single day.

There it was once again. That same cold-blooded, evil cruelty. As the prophet Jeremiah laments, "They acted shamefully because they committed abomination; they were not at all ashamed, they did not know how to blush" (Jeremiah 6:15) It was that same Manson-esque zombi-ism that controlled not just a cult following behind an empty reservoir, but an entire group of people living in Gaza. The cheering and excitement of what these "heroes" had accomplished. The exultation captured in text messages of the evil perpetrators to their parents.

And the world remained silent.

We cry out with King David, "How long shall the wicked, O G-d, how long shall the wicked exult? They gush forth and speak arrogantly, bearing themselves haughtily" (Psalms 94:3-4). Among the most gut-wrenching images of that day was the abduction of Shiri Bibas and her two cute, red-haired sons—Ariel, 4, and Kfir, just 9 months old—along with their father, Yarden. The image of Shiri, clutching her terrified children, should have seared itself into the world's conscience.

It didn't.

The anguish in her eyes, the tiny hands gripping her for protection. To us it was an image of raw, unfiltered horror. And yet, to the world, to those who just yesterday protested in Boro Park, to AOC, it meant nothing. Nada.

> "The wicked walk on every side, when vileness is exalted among the sons of men" (Psalms 12:9).

And yet, for all its gut-wrenching pain, this moment was only the beginning of their suffering.

For hundreds of agonizing days—we don't know the exact number—they remained in captivity. Subjected to the unknown torments of their captors. The world could only imagine the horror of their final moments. A mother, whose every instinct is to shield her children, powerless against the depraved inhumanity around her. [See below for the report of the Abu Kabir Forensic Institute regarding the deaths of the Bibas children.]

Where are you, leftist media? Where was and is the ICC? Where is UNWRA? The UN?

Silence. Cold deafening silence.

Ariel, a boy who should have been playing, his laughter filling a home, instead trapped in a nightmare. Kfir, a baby who had barely begun to experience life, held in his mother's arms, his cries unanswered. Their suffering defies comprehension. And when the news broke that they had been murdered, that the hope of their return had been extinguished, it was as though the breath had been stolen from all the Jewish People. But not the United Nations. Not the ICC.

"Do you indeed speak righteousness, O silent ones?" (Psalms 58:2).

No. Sadly, they do not. Just indifference.

The collective grief is immense. A sorrow weighs upon us all. An unbearable storm.

The images of Shiri and her children, once symbols of desperate hope, are now symbols of unbearable loss. When their bodies were finally released, their return was not a homecoming but a funeral procession, a final reminder of the cruelty that had stolen them away.

But then the evil, the depravity, reared its ugly head once again. They faked the body of Shiri—the mother. They replaced her body with an anonymous Gazan woman. The next day they admitted their vicious lie. How low can a human soul fall?

Prior to crossing into Israel, the army held a short ceremony during which Psalm 83 was read by the Chief Military Rabbi, Rav Eyal Karim. The IDF X-rayed the coffins as well. Streets filled with hearts heavy with sorrow, voices choked with tears. How can we find words for a crime so cruel? How does a people heal from a wound so deep?

In both the Manson murders and the October 7th massacre, the victims were not just killed; they were dehumanized before, during, and after their deaths. Manson's followers viewed their victims as symbols—representations of what they sought to destroy. Likewise, Hamas and its supporters dehumanized the Bibas family. To them, Ariel and Kfir were not a young toddler and a baby with giggles and dreams. They were not human beings.

One of the starkest contrasts between these two horrors lies in the aftermath. Manson and his followers were arrested, tried, and convicted. No ambiguity, no rationalization: Manson was evil—plain and simple. And he was treated as such. His crimes were condemned without hesitation, his name forever linked with the darkest recesses of human depravity.

Not so in the case of October 7th. There, moral clarity has eluded the world. The murder of Shiri Bibas and her children has been met with equivocation. With "context." An eerie silence from voices that claim to champion human rights.

The sheer inhumanity of their deaths has been diluted. Twisted.

The Manson murders were a wake-up call to America, a chilling reminder of the darkness that festers when extremism and dehumanization take hold. The October 7th massacre should be an even louder alarm. It should be a piercing siren demanding that we refuse to let ideology strip away moral clarity. The murder of Sharon Tate, the slaughter of the Bibas family—these are not just tragedies. They are indictments of the human capacity for evil. And they are warnings—warnings that history repeats itself when we fail to learn from its horrors.

The victims of these atrocities are more than names in history books. They were mothers, fathers, children. People with families. People who laughed. Who loved. Who dreamed.

To forget them, to excuse their suffering, is to allow the dark depravity that took them to spread. We must never let that happen. We must tell their stories, and we must demand that the world look into the abyss of these horrific crimes and have the courage to call them what they are. Pure and unadulterated evil.

Report from Abu Kabir Forensic Institute:

The terrorists strangled Kfir and Ariel to death, then brutally mutilated their bodies in an attempt to make it appear that they had been killed by the Israeli Air Force. Despite the horrific condition of the bodies, forensic investigators unanimously determined that Kfir and Ariel were cold-bloodedly murdered approximately ten days after October 7th, 2023.

"The world is a dangerous place to live not because most people are evil but because of the people who don't do anything about it." –Albert Einstein

"Hamas represents pure cruelty that must be met forcefully." –Isaac Herzog, President of Israel

The New 9/11

Gary Willig

NO DAY WAS more formative in my childhood than September 11, 2001. I remember my principal summoning the entire student body to the auditorium to tell us that a terrorist attack had been committed in lower Manhattan, but not providing any more details.

I remember the tears of a classmate who was terrified because his older sister went to college in Manhattan. I remember my father coming to pick me up during gym class and telling me in the car that the World Trade Center was no more and that thousands of people were dead. I remember the giant plume of dark purple smoke that cut through the otherwise clear blue skies during the drive home to Perth Amboy, New Jersey, and the knowledge that the world would never be the same again.

9/11 was a day I thought would never, could never happen again. Until October 7, 2023.

In Jerusalem, like in the rest of the country, we were celebrating the Simchat Torah holiday. The first sign that something was wrong was the Red Alert siren going off at about 8:15 am, just as I was about to leave for synagogue. The sound of the explosion of the Iron Dome system intercepting a rocket was quite loud, signaling that the rocket had been close to the Katamon neighborhood where I live.

On the way to synagogue, the first person I encountered on the street had not even heard the siren or the explosion. Others had. One person told me that the rocket had come from Gaza and not Lebanon, and for a while that was all I knew.

The prayer service I attended was supposed to be held on the roof of a local yeshiva, with outdoor Hakafot and a meat breakfast. Another siren went off at about 8:45, right as the service was supposed to begin, and we all went inside to wait for the siren to end. A third siren activated minutes later, and the decision was made to move the services entirely indoors.

The sirens continued to go off throughout the morning. There were numerous thuds from explosions caused by Iron Dome interceptions, but no more loud bangs from a close explosion like that first rocket attack. At one point, after the immediate danger had passed for the moment, we could see the white streaks of the Iron Dome interceptors on the path they had taken to save Israeli lives. The sight took me back to the cloud of 9/11, though while that dark cloud symbolized death and destruction, these white streaks symbolized life and resiliency.

No one at this prayer service knew exactly what was happening. We did not check our phones due to it being Shabbat and a yom tov (holiday). This many rocket attacks on the Jerusalem area obviously meant a very serious conflict was underway with the terrorist organizations in the Gaza Strip, but we had no way of knowing how bad it truly was. We knew that however bad it was in Jerusalem, in the south, in Sderot, in Ashkelon, and in all the communities near the Gaza border, it must have been a hundred times worse.

Make that a million times.

At about 11:30 am, while we were in the middle of reading from the Torah, the central part of the Simchat Torah services, a member of the yeshiva administration came in and told us that the order had been given to close all synagogues in Jerusalem and that we all had to go home. It was not just the rockets being fired at us, but there was intelligence that terrorists could infiltrate the city and synagogues where large numbers of Jews gathered would be prime targets. So we dispersed and concluded our prayers in private at home.

Once at home, there was no way to hear the instructions of Rabbi Shmuel Eliyahu, the Chief Rabbi of Safed, to keep our phones on. There was nothing to do but keep our doors locked and wait until the sun had set and Shabbat was over to learn the truth of what was happening.

After dark, we turned on the news. It was worse than I could ever have imagined.

Nothing could have prepared me for the headline: "Massive terror attack in Israel, more than 100 killed." Nothing could have prepared me for the details of this attack, that in addition to the expected thousands of rockets, Hamas had sent hundreds of terrorists across the border through and over the fence and even by sea to attack and murder Israelis in their cities, in their synagogues, in their homes, and in their sleep.

This was a long-planned and well-coordinated attack on Israel and the Jewish people's very existence, and a security and intelligence failure at least on par with the Egyptian and Syrian surprise attack at the start of the Yom Kippur War 50 years ago.

Just like on 9/11, the scale and magnitude of this terrorist attack are unimaginable. Just like on 9/11, the videos from the scene were horrifying, the sense of being under siege and at war was palpable. Just like that fateful day 22 years ago, nothing would ever be the same.

I thought 9/11 would never happen again. I should have known better. The same blind hatred, the same love and worship of death that led 19 men to take 3,000 lives in addition to their own, still exists. It can be seen in the videos of the captives, especially innocent civilians, being paraded through Gaza. It can be seen in the images of terrified families, children, and the elderly, hiding in protected areas of their homes or wailing for loved ones who were killed or taken captive.

We Jews have seen this evil before. We saw it in the massacres of Jewish communities in Europe during the crusades, in the pogroms of 19th Century Russia, and in the horrors of the Nazi Holocaust Genocide of 6 million men, women, and children for no other reason than that they are Jews.

We've seen it in the massacres of Darfur, Rwanda, and Xinjiang, and all the other mass murders That evil is constantly reborn every generation, now it lives in the hearts of the terrorists of Hamas and Hezbollah and their masters in Tehran. This kind of evil makes man do the bestial, the unthinkable, from flying passenger jets into skyscrapers to massacring Jews on their religious holidays.

Every victim has a name, friends, family, a life. The people who called their loved ones from the planes or from inside the towers before they fell that September morning gave voice to the fact that every one of the 3,000 victims of those attacks were more than numbers and statistics. They were human beings who endured horrors no one should ever have to face before their lives were cruelly snuffed out.

It is the same with the victims of Hamas' barbarism. As of the writing of this piece, the death toll is over 500. That is 500 lives snuffed out, 500 worlds ended. 500 stories suddenly stopped in the middle. And for what? Not in any fight for freedom, but in a fight to ensure that Jews have no rights, not the right to self-determination, and not the right to live.

So much has changed since September 11, 2001. I am no longer an elementary school pupil, blissfully unaware of the evil of those who worship death and hate those they call "infidels.". But against this kind of evil, there is little one person can do. It takes a nation, a world even, to stand up to the evil of Hamas and Iran, as the United States once stood up to Japan and the Nazis after Pearl Harbor. It will take all of us, standing together, to defeat this evil and ensure that this time, it cannot happen. October 7, 2023 must be the last 9/11.

May the Almighty guard and protect the brave soldiers who are risking their lives to protect their loved ones and fellow citizens and in defense of life itself. May He speedily deliver the captives from their captivity. May the souls of the slain find peace and tranquility in heaven, their names and stories never forgotten by the living. May their murderers rot forever in the pits of hell where they will go. And may the name of Hamas and all like it, Al Qaeda, Islamic State, and Hezbollah, be blotted out so those who love life and peace no longer have to fear those who love and worship death above all else.

Chapter Four

Psychopathology of Sexual Abuse

Genocidal rape is a heinous crime that goes beyond physical violence to inflict deep psychological and social wounds on victims and their communities. Understanding the psychopathology behind it helps us recognize the calculated and strategic nature of these atrocities. By acknowledging and confronting the realities of genocidal rape, we can better support survivors and their families, protect future generations, and work toward justice and healing.

The Women's Movement Has a Double Standard When Sexual Violence Happens to Jews

Meredith Jacobs

"Do you want to talk about what just happened in Israel?"
I didn't have to think for very long.

"No," I responded to the email. "I don't think this group is a safe space."

On October 12, I joined a regular scheduled Zoom call with major women's rights organizations, as I have done since the group was founded.

The coordinator, who happens to be Jewish, began the call by asking for a moment to recognize the horrific terrorist attack that had just occurred in Israel. She asked those gathered to think about their Jewish colleagues and the pain they are in.

Her comments were met with silence. Had this very same terrorist attack happened to any other group, any other people, the Zoom chat would have been filled with messages of sympathy, shared pain, offers to stand together and to help amplify messages.

But none of that happened. No "heart" reactions appeared on the squares of those with whom we have sat in coalition and in sisterhood for years. No messages of support or care came through in the chat. I received no private messages asking if we were OK.

Finally, I wrote "thank you" in the chat. The other Jewish organization participating did the same. That was the last time I participated in the calls.

I thought the silence was bad enough. I never expected what would come next — denial.

There is abundant evidence that Hamas and other terrorists committed horrifying acts of sexual violence on Oct. 7. Sexual violence has unfortunately been a part of armed conflict for thousands of years, and it is used to humiliate and degrade both individuals and their broader communities.

There is no reason to think that the terrorists who infiltrated southern Israel on Oct. 7 would act any differently from generations of invaders who came before them. And yet, many women's rights organizations are going out of their way to deny the horrific violence done to Jewish women.

A rape crisis center at Canada's University of Alberta earlier this month signed onto an open letter, which includes the idea that calling Hamas terrorists is Islamophobic and denies that Israeli women were raped by Hamas.

For those of us who work to end domestic and sexual violence, there are two key tenets: Believe women. And never blame the victim. This letter — and I cannot stress this enough, coming from a rape crisis center — managed to go against both.

Advocates who work with survivors know that not being believed, or being called a liar deserving of the violence, is retraumatizing for victims, and silences others who might come forward.

And yet here we were. The brutal rapes, bodily mutilations, and sadistic murder of women and children on Oct. 7 is being dismissed as lies and Zionist propaganda.

Why are these crimes OK when they happen to Israeli

bodies? To Jewish bodies?

In 2008, the United Nations' Security Council declared rape a war crime. In 2017, Angelina Jolie, then special envoy to the UN., urged the UN to do more to prevent and punish sexual violence during war. She explained that sexual violence, "is cheaper than a bullet, and it has lasting consequences that unfold with sickening predictability that make it so cruelly effective."

Where is Angelia Jolie now that crimes have been committed against Israeli women and children? Where, for that matter, is the UN?

As has been widely reported, the UN — and specifically, the United Nations' Committee on the Elimination of Discrimination against Women — failed to immediately condemn the mass raping of Israeli women and girls by Hamas. Instead, they waited 49 days, and then did so only after a viral condemnation by Sheryl Sandberg, multiple news reports, and a global social media campaign calling out UN Women and other women's organizations for their double standards. Even then, the "statement" by UN Women (really a post on the social media network formerly known as Twitter) said the following:

> We met with Israeli women's organizations & heard about the work of the Civil Commission for crimes against women & children.
>
> We remain alarmed by gender-based violence reports on 7 Oct & call for rigorous investigation, prioritizing the rights, needs & safety of those affected.

They remain silent about the hostages. Silent on the

urgent care the rape victims need. Silent on protecting them from further assault.

Silent.

Instead, they call for "rigorous investigation" — not believing the victims by calling for further proof before taking a stance. They also failed to name the victims as Israeli women, instead writing "those affected."

We know what happened. Survivors of the Nova Festival have reported in graphic detail witnessing a gang rape. Those who have handled the bodies of the deceased report broken pelvic bones and horrific bodily mutilation. There was a widely shown video on multiple news channels of a young woman being shoved into a jeep, the seat of her sweatpants soaked in her blood. Those of us who bore witness to the raw footage, publicized by Hamas and then shown to us by the IDF, saw additional videos, some taken by the GoPro cameras worn by the terrorists, of women and young girls lying on the ground or tied to beds, undergarments around their ankles. We saw footage of naked women being dragged through the streets of Gaza City, trophies of war, to be kicked, spat upon, and worse.

No decent person wants civilians to be harmed, no matter what nationality they may be. The world should condemn the violence perpetrated against Israeli women and children — no more, but certainly no less, than they have and would do for any other people.

After I watched the 45-minute reel of raw footage at the Embassy of Israel in Washington, D.C., I spoke with Michal Cotler-Wunsh, a former Member of Knesset and now Israel's Special Envoy for Combating Antisemitism. She explained that the silence, especially by those who would speak out for victims from any other community, is made possible by the three Ds of antisemitism — dehumanization, delegitimization, and double standards.

I am haunted by Shylock's line from Shakespeare's *The Merchant of Venice*, "If you prick us, do we not bleed?" I didn't appreciate the line or the sentiment when I first read the book in high school, but now the cry to be recognized as human is prescient. And painful.

Though my organization focuses on many critical women's issues, we take a particularly active role in combatting domestic and sexual violence. For those who have called and emailed and asked me, because of my position and the mission of Jewish Women International, to explain what is happening, I have no charitable explanation. My only explanation is hate.

For those who ask me how I'm feeling or what we can do, my answer is that we must keep talking about and calling out the hypocrisy and double standards. We can keep crying for justice and for those in positions of power to speak out.

We must keep demanding that the horrific crimes committed against Israeli women and girls be condemned in the same full-throated way by those who decry the plight of women and children in Gaza.

In an Oct. 23 letter written after the Oct. 20 report by UN Women on the "devastating impact of the crisis in Gaza on women and girls," which neglected to mention how Israeli women were also brutalized, seven Israeli women, all experts in international crime and violence against women, condemned the double standards:

> As reputable international bodies charged with the protection of all human beings, and in particular the most vulnerable, we expect an unequivocal

condemnation of [the Oct. 7 atrocities committed against Israeli women and children] without equating them with what is now happening in Gaza, tragic as that is.

They went on to explain that what is happening in Gaza is "a tragic war." But what happened in Israel on Oct. 7 is "evil incarnate" and, like the massacres under Nazi rule, "must be condemned without equivocation."

When the letter went unanswered, Dr. Elkayam-Levy, executive director of the Deborah Institute and adjunct professor on gender, peace, and security at Reichman University, founded the Civil Commission on Oct. 7 Crimes by Hamas Against Women and Children, focusing her energy full time on collecting evidence of the crimes.

This is not an easy task. Many of the victims' bodies were burned or have been buried. But this is where we are now: collecting the evidence of horrific crimes, crimes with video proof, with testimony of witnesses — because for some reason, the proof that would be enough for anyone else is not enough for us.

I fear none of this work will change minds. That nothing I or anyone else will say will make a difference.

I am overwhelmed by a sense of aloneness in the world. But even if what we say will not make a difference, we must continue to tell the simple reality: Violence against Jewish bodies, Israeli bodies, is a crime against humanity.

The world might ignore it. But that doesn't make it any less true.

The True Face of Israel's Enemies: The Roots of Psychopathological Sexual Abuse

Moshe Kaplan, MD

Hamas's Strategy for Creating a False Perception of Reality

Hamas has become adept at manipulating reality to serve its purposes. This manipulation is not just about spreading falsehoods but also about crafting a narrative that garners international sympathy, deflects criticism, and paints Israel as the villain. While Israel has made significant efforts to counteract this strategy through public relations, social media engagement, and diplomatic channels, the challenges remain formidable. The ongoing battle for hearts and minds is a crucial aspect of the broader conflict, and understanding the psychological tactics at play is essential if we are to comprehend the complexities of Israel's struggle for survival. As the war continues, Hamas will undoubtedly continue to vie for control over the narrative, seeking to win support and justify its actions on the global stage. The persistent media bias, entrenched public perceptions, and cultural divides make it difficult for Israel to shift this narrative. Understanding and addressing these challenges is crucial so that Israel can effectively counter Hamas's propaganda and present the reality of the conflict to the world. Let's dive into how Hamas creates these false perceptions and the psychology behind it. We'll also look at what Israel has done over the years to counteract this strategy, what has worked, and what hasn't.

The Art of Deception

Hamas employs a variety of tactics to distort the reality of the conflict:

Hamas spreads misleading information and sensationalized images through various media channels. This includes exaggerating or fabricating casualty figures, making false claims that Israeli forces have committed mass rape, staging incidents to elicit emotional responses, and spreading doctored or out-of-context images and videos. These stories, which international media often pick up without verification, skew public perception against Israel.

Captured terrorists have confessed to intentionally spreading deceitful propaganda, such as the story about the explosion at the Al-Ahli Al-Ma'mdani Hospital, which was caused by an Islamic Jihad rocket but blamed on Israel. Hamas used this intentional misinformation to deceive both Arab and international media.

Hamas's *modus operandus* is to place military operations strategically within civilian areas, such as schools, hospitals, and residential buildings. This ensures that when Israel retaliates, Hamas can showcase any civilian casualties as evidence of Israeli brutality. Hamas employs this tactic to invoke international outrage against Israel while obscuring its own responsibility for these deaths.

Tariq Salami Otha Abu Shlouf, a spokesperson for Islamic Jihad, admitted under interrogation that terror groups use hospitals as military bases because of their constant supply of internet and electricity. He also revealed that terrorists disguise themselves in civilian clothing to blend in, which is a war crime.

Using platforms like Twitter and Facebook, Hamas spreads its narrative rapidly and widely. The immediacy and emotional impact of social media posts allow Hamas to shape global perceptions quickly, often outpacing Israel's efforts to present the facts.

The Psychological Underpinnings Behind Hamas's Strategy

Understanding why Hamas's tactics work involves delving into psychological principles.

By positioning itself as the perpetual victim, Hamas taps into global sympathies. People tend to empathize with the perceived underdog, and Hamas's narrative of suffering and oppression against a powerful Israeli state fits neatly into this psychological framework, especially when amplified with emotional imagery and staged testimonials.

The use of graphic images and emotionally charged stories plays on the emotions of fear and anger, which are central to Hamas's propaganda. Graphic images of injured children, destroyed homes, and grieving families evoke strong emotional responses, overshadowing rational analysis and making it easier for people to accept distorted realities, encouraging a bias against Israel.

Hamas fosters a strong sense of identity among Palestinians while demonizing Israelis. This in-group/out-group dichotomy simplifies the conflict into a moral struggle, simultaneously rallying support from the Palestinians and making it easier for international audiences to take sides.

Though we have shown that Hamas has perfected the art of creating a false perception of reality as a sophisticated and deeply psychological tactic designed to garner international sympathy and vilify Israel, Hamas does not stand alone. To truly understand the dynamics at play, it's crucial to take a closer look at the actions and ideologies of all those perpetuating violence and chaos. Examining the true nature of the entities that are facilitating and backing Israel's enemies, including the Palestinian Authority (PA), United Nations Relief and Works Agency (UNRWA), and their supporters, will reveal the often-hidden truths behind their strategies and intentions.

The Palestinian Authority: Complicity in Terrorism

While Hamas often takes the spotlight, the Palestinian Authority (PA) also plays a significant role in perpetuating anti-Israel sentiments and supporting terrorist activities. The PA frequently glorifies terrorists and their acts. For instance, Muna Al-Khalili, the new PA Minister of Women's Affairs, has publicly praised terrorist attacks and called for continued resistance against Israel. Her support for individuals like Dalal Mughrabi, who led a deadly bus hijacking that killed 37 civilians, exemplifies the PA's endorsement of violence as a legitimate form of "resistance."

PA-run schools often use textbooks that glorify jihad and martyrdom while erasing Israel from their maps. This indoctrination starts from a young age, ensuring that future generations will grow up with a deep-seated hatred of Israel and Jews. This systemic brainwashing perpetuates the cycle of violence and makes any potential peace process more challenging.

International Enablers: UNRWA and Beyond

Further compounding the issue of Hamas's manipulated truths and propaganda is the role of the United Nations Relief and Works Agency (UNRWA). Established to provide aid to Palestinian refugees, UNRWA has long been implicated in aiding Hamas's propaganda efforts.

UNRWA has a unique approach among United Nations agencies. It grants perpetual refugee status to Palestinians, while other UN agencies seek to resettle those displaced by war or violence. A JNS investigation revealed that UNRWA does not revoke the refugee status of Palestinian terrorists, a stark contrast to the practices of the UN High Commissioner for Refugees (UNHCR), which excludes individuals involved in acts of terrorism elsewhere from refugee status.

Investigations have revealed that at least twelve UNRWA employees participated in the October 7th massacre, and that many more have ties to Hamas. Despite these alarming connections, UNRWA has been reluctant to take significant action against these employees. The agency's Commissioner-General, Philippe Lazzarini, admitted that it terminated some staff members' positions, in order to protect the agency's ability to deliver humanitarian assistance, but he did not address the deeper issue of UNRWA's systemic involvement with Hamas.

UNRWA schools use textbooks that glorify violent jihad as a noble pursuit, erase the existence of Israel from their maps, praise the martyrdom of Palestinian terrorists, and dehumanize Jews and Israelis. This indoctrination is a significant factor in the perpetuation of Hamas's extremist mindset, with the radicalization of young minds having a profound impact on the generations of Gazans who attended UNRWA schools, many of whom participated in the October 7th attacks.

The Reality of Radicalization

The story of Yaron Avraham, a former jihadist-in-training who converted to Judaism, provides a stark illustration of the radicalization process and the possibility of change. Yaron's journey from being indoctrinated in a Gaza mosque to becoming a committed Jew and IDF soldier highlights the intense psychological manipulation young Palestinians endure and the potential for redemption and transformation through exposure to different perspectives and values.

In addition, documents revealed by *The London Times* show that Iran has provided hundreds of millions of dollars to Hamas, financing its military operations against Israel. This financial support underscores the deep connections between Hamas and Iranian interests, further complicating the geopolitical landscape.

The Horrors of Genocidal Rape: Understanding the Psychopathology Behind It

Moshe Kaplan, MD

When we talk about the atrocities committed during wartime, genocidal rape stands out as one of the most horrific. This isn't a random act of violence; it's a calculated, strategic use of sexual violence to terrorize, humiliate, and destroy entire communities. It isn't just about sexual gratification either; it's about power, domination, and a twisted form of warfare.

In order to understand what genocidal rape truly is, we must understand the psychology behind it, as well as its devastating impact on victims and societies.

Genocidal rape is a horrifying strategy used in wars to terrorize and break down communities. It's not an accidental by-product of conflict but a deliberate tactic aimed at destroying a targeted group. History is sadly full of examples of genocidal rape, which happened in numerous conflicts such as the Armenian Genocide, the Holocaust, the Bosnian War, and the Rwandan Genocide.

During the Armenian Genocide, Turkish soldiers raped and killed Armenian women and children during forced marches. Women were often taken as sex slaves or forced into marriages where they were compelled to convert to Islam.

In the Rwandan Genocide, it's estimated that Hutu soldiers raped between 250,000 and 500,000 women and girls as a tactic of war. Survivors often found themselves stigmatized and ostracized, and many also discovered that they were infected with HIV. The goal was not just to terrorize but to destroy the social fabric of the Tutsi community.

In Bosnia, during the ethnic cleansing campaigns, Serbian forces used mass rape as a deliberate strategy to ethnically cleanse the region of its Muslim population. Serbian forces used rape to force impregnation so that Bosnian Muslim women would bear Serbian children. It was a cruel way to ensure the destruction of the Bosnian Muslim community's identity and cause long-term damage to the community's future.

Power and domination play a huge role. Perpetrators use rape to exert control and dominance over their victims. It lets them demonstrate their power and demoralize the enemy. In many cases, rape is about showing absolute power over the most intimate and personal aspects of a victim's life.

Humiliation and dehumanization are also key objectives. Rape in this context is used to strip victims of their dignity and humanity. In many cultures, rape carries severe social stigma, leading to ostracization and isolation. This doesn't affect just the individual but it also fractures families and communities.

The impact of genocidal rape is profound and long-lasting. Victims suffer from severe physical injuries and psychological trauma, including PTSD, depression, and other mental health disorders. The stigma attached to rape often prevents survivors from seeking help, exacerbating their suffering.

Socially, the stigma can lead to victims being ostracized, disrupting the social fabric of their communities. This isolation can prevent survivors from reintegrating into society, leading to long-term economic and social disadvantages. The forced pregnancies resulting from these rapes bring additional challenges. Children born from rape often face identity crises and social stigma, becoming living reminders of the trauma their mothers endured.

Multiple Perpetrator Rape: A Deeper Look into the Origins of Hamas's Behavior

Moshe Kaplan, MD

ANOTHER HORRIFYING DIMENSION of sexual violence in conflict is multiple perpetrator rape (MPR). This form of sexual violence involves gang rapes in which several individuals participate, often in an orchestrated manner. The psychology behind MPR is complex and deeply disturbing.

One of the leading theories to explain MPR is the Multi-Factorial Theory of Multiple Perpetrator Sexual Offending, which Leigh Harkins and Louise Dixon developed in 2010. This theory suggests that a combination of individual, socio-cultural, and situational factors contribute to MPR. It's a more comprehensive approach than earlier theories, which often focused on just one of these aspects.

Group dynamics play a crucial role in MPR. The presence of a group leader or instigator is often pivotal. This leader can influence the behavior of other group members, encouraging them to participate in the assault. The need for group cohesion and peer acceptance can drive individuals to commit acts they might not have considered alone.

In many cases, the group process reduces personal

inhibitions and creates a sense of anonymity among the perpetrators. This deindividuation can lead to behavior that is more extreme and violent than any that an individual would normally exhibit. The group setting also diffuses responsibility, making it easier for individuals to justify their actions as part of a collective effort.

The socio-cultural context, including norms and beliefs about gender and power, also plays a significant role. In some cultures, rape myths and patriarchal values can normalize sexual violence and make it more likely to occur in a group setting. Situational factors, such as the presence of alcohol or the chaotic environment of war, can further exacerbate these tendencies.

Research shows that MPR often occurs in environments where violent and hyper-masculine norms are prevalent. This is particularly evident in military and paramilitary groups that prize aggression and dominance, and who use sexual violence as a tool to assert power and control over the enemy.

It is impossible to overstate the horrific psychological impact on the victims of MPR. The trauma is magnified by the fact that multiple individuals perpetrate the violence, often leading to severe physical injuries, long-term psychological damage, and intense feelings of humiliation and dehumanization.

In addition to personal suffering, the societal impact of MPR is devastating. The after-effects tear communities apart, as trust and social cohesion erode. The use of rape as a weapon of war instills fear and helplessness, making it difficult for communities to rebuild and recover. The long-term psychological scars affect not just the direct victims but also future generations who grow up in an environment shaped by violence and trauma.

The World Looks Away

Moshe Kaplan, MD

"I RAPED HER," a captured Hamas terrorist describes on film as he's interrogated by Israeli security forces. He was one of thousands of fighters who entered Israel with "intentions to kidnap as many, to rape as many, to humiliate as many, to murder as many" Israelis as possible, reports Mirit Ben Mayor, Chief Superintendent of Israel Police. She has sifted through 200,000 photos and videos, and 2,000 witness testimonies. "We have substantial evidence for sexual violence that took place on the 7th of October," she says.

Raz Cohen, a young man who was at the Nova Music Festival, survived by hiding in bushes with his friend, Shoham. He described Shoham saying, "'He's stabbing her. He's slaughtering her'... I didn't want to look... When I looked again, she was already dead, and he was still at it. He was still raping her after he had slaughtered her."

Amit Soussana, a young woman who was held hostage in Gaza for 55 days, has described the moment she was sexually assaulted by her captor, Mohammed. Michal Ohana, a young woman who was severely injured at the Nova Festival and left for dead for seven hours describes the scene. "I realized that they [Hamas] hadn't just come here to murder" but also to sexually assault women. Volunteers with ZAKA, Israel's famed search and rescue organization, describe witnessing many dead bodies after the attack that bore signs of unimaginable sexual violence.

Tali Binner is a young woman who attended the Nova Music Festival. Tali and two friends hid in a camper during Hamas's rampage. Tali describes hearing women's screams all around her. "I heard a girl that started to yell for a long time. It was like, 'Please don't. No, no, stop, stop, stop, no, no...'" One by one, Tali recounted, the voices of the victims around her went silent as the attackers shot each woman after raping her.

United Nations Secretary General Antonio Guterres all but publicly declared that Hamas had not used sexual violence. His annual report on "Conflict-related Sexual Violence" pointedly refused to list Hamas as an organization that employed sexual violence during the period that included October 7, 2023.

This omission was all the more surprising given the existence of an internal UN report, issued March 11, 2024, that found evidence of Hamas's "rape and gang rape" on October 7. Secretary General Guterres refusal to acknowledge Hamas's sexual violence echoes a widespread effort to deny that there was any rape or weaponization of sexual assaults.

On December 8, 2023, *The New York Times* published an in-depth investigation into Hamas's widespread and systematic use of sexual violence on October 7. It found that Hamas's "attacks against women were not isolated events but part of a broader pattern of gender-based violence on October 7." That report prompted a revolt inside the *Times*, with some reporters complaining that the story reflected an anti-Arab bias within the newsroom.

Prominent far-left journalists also attacked the story. The influential site, *The Intercept,* was so eager to assert that Hamas hadn't engaged in rape that it airily assured readers that "rape is not uncommon in war," and posited that ordinary civilians, not Hamas fighters, must have been responsible for any sexual assaults. The influential British journalist Owen Jones even went to the trouble of creating his own online video claiming that there is "no evidence" that Hamas engaged in sexual violence; the video has garnered over 624,000 views.

Women's Groups Defending Hamas

Rather than attacking Hamas for its systematic and deliberate use of sexual violence as a tool of war, many global women's organizations have placed their allegiance to a radical anti-Israel view above their duty to speak out against violence against women.

Take Gender Studies departments in universities around the world. In 2021, over 120 Gender Studies departments signed a joint statement denouncing Israel and committing their definition of "feminist vision" to a radical view of Palestinian opposition to the Jewish state. In the aftermath of the October 7 attacks, not a single Gender Studies department criticized Hamas's use of sexual violence in the attack.

UN Women, the United Nations body responsible for safeguarding women's rights around the world, has similarly refrained from singling out Hamas's use of sexual violence for opprobrium. After issuing a condemnation of the "brutal attacks by Hamas on Israel on 7 October," it later replaced even that feeble critique on its website with a bland statement decrying "attacks on civilians in Israel and the Occupied Palestinian Territories." It's shocking that the very people we charge with safeguarding the safety and dignity of women can so easily dismiss horrific gender-based violence when it's Israeli Jews who are the victims.

A recent new poll revealed that nearly a tenth of young Americans today report feeling that the *way* Hamas carried out the October 7 attacks is acceptable. This, despite the fact that they had seen news reports presenting the horrific stories of rape and sexual sadism.

Israeli legal scholar Prof. Ruth Halperin-Kaddari notes that Hamas's attacks on women on October 7 was no accident. Hamas used rape and sexual sadism as a deliberate "tool of war.... Because when the body of the woman is violated, it symbolizes the whole nation." Hamas's merciless targeting of Jewish women's bodies was an attack on the entire Jewish nation.

Silent Cry: Sexual Crimes in the October 7 War

Special Report of the Association of Rape Crisis Centers in Israel

Authors:
Research and Writing: Karmit Klar-Chalamish, PhD
Editing: Noga Berger, together with the
ARCCI production team and staff

This report was published with the generous support of: Women's Amutot Initiative of the Greater Miami Jewish Federation, Charles and Lynn Schusterman Family Foundation, and The Harry and Jeanette Weinberg Foundation.

Content Warning: The report contains graphic descriptions of sexual abuse, torture, and murder.

Abstract

Hamas's attack on October 7 included brutal sexual assaults, carried out systematically and deliberately toward Israeli civilians. Numerous testimonies and pieces of disclosed and classified information present a clear picture of identical patterns of action repeated in each of the attack zones — the Nova Festival, private homes in the Gaza envelope kibbutzim, and IDF bases. With the abduction of 254 individuals to the Gaza Strip areas, sexual assaults continued to occur also in this arena. Therefore, there is a high likelihood that the kidnapped women and men in Hamas captivity are still at risk of sexual abuse at any given moment.

Hamas's attack included violent acts of rape, accompanied by threats with weapons, and in some cases targeted toward injured women. Many of the rapes were carried out as a group, with the participation of violent terrorists. Often, the rape was perpetrated in front of an audience — partners, family, or friends — in a manner intended to increase the pain and humiliation of all present. Hamas terrorists hunted young women and men who fled the Nova Festival, and according to testimonies, dragged them by their hair amid screams. The actions targeted women, girls, and men. In most cases, the victims were killed after or even during the rape.

A series of testimonies, interviews, and additional sources attest that Hamas terrorists employed sadistic practices aimed at intensifying the degree of humiliation and terror inherent in sexual violence. Many of the bodies of sexual crime victims were found bound and shackled. The genitals of both women and men were brutally mutilated, and sometimes weapons were inserted into them. The terrorists did not stop at shooting; they also cut and mutilated sexual organs and other body parts with knives.

This report is the result of an initial examination of all the public and classified information, interviews, and testimonies that can be revealed at this time, which will likely increase with time. The report clearly demonstrates that sexual abuse was not an isolated incident or sporadic cases but rather a clear operational strategy.

Those who choose to remain silent, silence others, or deny the sexual crimes committed by Hamas will be remembered accordingly.

Opening Remarks

Orit Sulitzeanu, Executive Director — The Association of Rape Crisis Centers in Israel

2024. Seven years since the #MeToo movement erupted, a quarter of a century after the Kosovo War in which the use of sexual violence in warfare entered public discourse, decades of feminist struggle to break the walls of silence and denial surrounding sexual assault — and the world is silent once again.

Against this incomprehensible silence, the Association of Rape Crisis Centers in Israel (ARCCI) released the report before you, which examines the sexual and gender-based violence perpetrated in the massacre of October 7, 2023 and the war that ensued.

The information and testimonies we provide clarify beyond any doubt what occurred, but significant parts of the story are still ahead of us. Since sexual assault typically involves delayed disclosure, especially during wartime, the picture presented in the report is still preliminary. In the months and years to come, depending on the choices of the survivors, we may be able to bring a fuller story of the sexual assaults on October 7 and thereafter to the fore.

Introduction

On Saturday, October 7, 2023, at 06:29 AM, during the festive holiday of Simchat Torah, Hamas initiated a sudden attack on Israel from the Gaza Strip. Under heavy rocket fire, thousands of militants infiltrated into Israeli territory. They entered homes in kibbutzim surrounding Gaza while family members were asleep in their beds or sheltering in safe rooms; they raided nature parties taking place in the area; seized control of IDF bases, and particularly targeted IDF observation posts with unarmed women soldiers in position. Over 1,200 people were killed in a single day, the vast majority of whom were civilians, and 254 Israeli and foreign citizens were abducted to the Gaza Strip, including women, men, children, babies, and the elderly.

Immediately following the massacre, numerous accounts began to emerge about sexual offenses that occurred during it. The testimonies came from all locations of the attack — homes, the Nova Festival, and IDF bases. Subsequently, with the release of some of the kidnapped women, testimonies about sexual violence in captivity also surfaced, crimes which may be continuing to occur even as these lines are being written.

This special report focuses on the sexual and gender-based offenses committed during the war. It offers an analysis of testimonies and information about the events by the Association of Rape Crisis Centers in Israel, as can be presented at this point in time (February 2024, four months after the outbreak of the war). This serves as initial evidence of systematic and widespread sexual crimes.

Dealing with sexual and gender-based violence during

war inherently involves a tension between society and the individual. For society, there is historical, national, and international significance in acknowledging the atrocities that occurred. Faced with denial that began immediately with the emergence of the first accounts, there is an acute need for explanations and concrete descriptions in words that can break the bond of silence and silencing. This is especially poignant as many of those who have been raped and tortured were murdered, unable to ever voice their experiences. When most of the victims of sexual assaults are murdered, we have a moral and humanitarian obligation to amplify their silent cry.

On the other hand, no survivor should feel obligated to "serve" the world's demand for information. The choice of whether to speak, what to disclose, when, and how should be theirs. Typically, sexual violence in "normal" circumstances is characterized by delayed disclosure, with most cases not reported until months, years, or even decades later, and sometimes never. Experience worldwide indicates that in times of war, disclosure is even further delayed. This process of maturation must not be hastened. After their bodies have been violated, survivors must be allowed to regain control, which may include telling their stories at a time that is appropriate for them.

Throughout the writing process, we aimed to uphold this complexity. At any point of uncertainty, we acted according to the ethical principles of the rape crisis centers, which prioritize the preferences and choices of the survivors at the forefront. Consequently, we cannot present in this document all the information and accounts that have come to us confidentially. Nevertheless, we have made an effort to provide a picture of the situation that reflects information from open sources (primarily) as well as information that we cannot fully disclose at this stage.

About the Association of Rape Crisis Centers in Israel

The Association of Rape Crisis Centers in Israel (ARCCI) was founded in 1990 as an umbrella organization, uniting nine rape crisis centers spread across the country that receive approximately 50,000 inquiries each year. The rape crisis centers for victims and survivors of sexual assault operate on an individual level and provide a wide range of services for survivors of sexual violence, including immediate psychological support, support groups, assistance in legal and medical processes, advocacy, and more. These services are offered to victims and survivors from all sectors of Israeli society, to family members, and to professional teams. In addition, the rape crisis centers work within their local communities and in partnership with ARCCI, operating education, awareness, and prevention programs.

The Association of Rape Crisis Centers in Israel acts as an agent for social change at both the national and systemic levels, complementing and relying on the individual work carried out in the rape crisis centers. The association works to promote rights and services for survivors of sexual assault, to adopt preventive and systemic treatment measures, and to reduce the incidence of the phenomenon in Israel. The association's activities include, among others, promoting policy and legislation, fundamental legal proceedings, shaping public discourse on the phenomenon of sexual violence, research, and the collection and dissemination of knowledge.

The diverse services provided by the centers and the association are the result of over three decades of experience, during which time saw the creation of a professional body of knowledge and expertise regarding sexual violence in general, its characteristics, and its implications for the lives of victims and survivors, and for society as a whole.

Following October 7, the ARCCI jointly established the "Lilach Project: Access to justice for the Victims of October 7," an initiative aimed at ensuring the rights (both existing and new) of the massacre victims and their families, adapting the rights to the unique situation and ensuring trauma-informed implementation. The project was initiated by Prof. Dana Pugach, in collaboration with The Hostages and Missing Families Forum, and named after Lilach Kipnis, a social worker and volunteer at the Negev Rape Crisis center (Maslan), who was murdered with her family on that fateful Black Saturday.

Background: Sexual Crimes in War

Sexual violence during armed conflicts, both national and international, is explicitly defined as war crimes prohibited by the Rome Statute (1998). The statute established the jurisdiction of the International Criminal Court (ICC) to act in cases of sexual crimes in wartime.

Characteristics

In the literature, several unique parameters defining sexual violence in war are identified, ones that influence in the short and long-term:[1]

- Life-threatening situations: Sexual violence during wartime is predominantly perpetrated by soldiers or armed forces against unarmed civilians. In these circumstances, sexual violence is linked to a direct threat to life.
- Reporting: The prevalence of sexual assaults and rape during war and captivity is particularly high. However, these offenses are also characterized by significant underreporting, both due to difficulties in reporting (such as shame, fear of social stigma and retaliation, etc.) and the fact that a significant portion of the victims are killed or die afterward.
- Proliferation of gang rapes: Estimates suggest that around 90% of wartime rapes are gang rapes committed in the presence and participation of multiple perpetrators.[2] The collective perpetration strengthens bonds and solidarity among the perpetrators.
- Sexual violence in the presence of others: In addition to gang rapes and sexual attacks committed in the presence of other perpetrators, sexual violence during war is often perpetrated in the presence of other women to instill fear, or in the presence of family members and other community members to demonstrate and deepen oppression and humiliation. Rape of a partner or family member aims to expand the humiliation to bystanders who remain powerless or suffer additional violence in attempts to stop it. Another exertion of control is when one of the family members is forced to rape another family member. Dragging women out of their homes to the sound of their screams is a way to harm the community and exert control over the

enemy through psychological and physical means. In the current era, the use of media and social networks — distributing videos depicting atrocities — allows for spreading fear to a wider audience, beyond those physically present.
- Brutality: Wartime rape often occurs alongside practices of sadism, xenophobia, and dehumanization. Rape during wartime is characterized by dehumanization, where the woman in front of the perpetrator is not considered human but rather a symbolic body subjected to hatred and violence. Brutality is also manifested in the physical injuries accompanying sexual violence during wartime.
- Characteristics of slavery and subjugation: During wartime, we see women held in captivity and subjected to sexual assault and rape. Women and young girls are held in "rape camps" where they undergo torture, verbal abuse, and intensive rape.

These parameters provide a framework for understanding the nature and impact of sexual violence in wartime, highlighting the need for comprehensive responses to address the complex challenges posed by such crimes.

Implications

Survivors in need of help in their healing journey after the offense they suffered during wartime often struggle to receive the necessary treatment or support they require because their environments are often focused on rebuilding and survival rather than on addressing the needs of those who experienced sexual violence.

Sexual trauma in war occurs within the context of larger, complex emergency situations, which include the destruction of political, economic, socio-cultural, and health infrastructures.[3] Often, the survivors and their families must cope with the displacement of their communities and the need to resettle.

Psychological Implications

Sexual assault during war is characterized by a loss of control over the body, similar to other forms of sexual assault, but also by a loss of one's basic sense of security and control over all aspects of life.

Women who have experienced sexual assault during war may experience PTSD, general anxiety, sleep disturbances, flashbacks, nightmares, and depression. Other possible consequences include disinterest in the environment, loss of self-esteem, hopelessness, self-loathing, body dissociation, and self-harm.[4]

The consequences may also include intentional isolation by survivors who impose on themselves distance due to fear of stigma, shame, rejection, or negative responses.[5]

Physical Implications

Women who have experienced rape during wartime may also suffer from physical traumas, including vaginal and rectal injuries, tears and lacerations, throat injuries (as a result of forced oral sex), fractures, and broken bones.

The medical consequences of sexual trauma can include sexually transmitted infections (such as HIV), sexual dysfunction, reproductive disorders, carcinoma, narcotic addiction, chronic infections, as well as more "common" somatic symptoms such as back pain, headaches, fatigue, dizziness, insomnia, chronic pelvic pain, hormonal dysfunction, gastrointestinal pain, and eating disorders.

Medical treatment during and after wartime may be limited or impossible; there may be difficulties in treating injuries due to unsanitary conditions, shortages of supplies and medications, inadequate medical facilities, and the victims' difficulty in reporting or disclosing the injury. As a result, women who have been sexually assaulted during war often face long-term health problems.[6]

Methodology

To prepare this report, dozens of pieces of information related to the commission of sexual and gender crimes were examined. Various pieces of information were collected from official sources, publications in local and international press, interviews with "first responders" in different arenas, as well as information that arrived at the ARCCI from professionals and confidential calls. Information from social networks or unverified sources was not included.

After locating the information, a process of cataloging and analysis was conducted to map out the areas and patterns of operation of the incidents in which sexual crimes were committed. As stated in the introduction to this report, direct accounts of what occurred and shared with the ARCCI team as part of its work will not be included. However, efforts were made to reflect these matters in the analysis itself.

On the Process of Collecting Evidence: "But why aren't they speaking?"

The difficulty in disclosing sexual assault is a well-known and recognized characteristic of the phenomenon even in times of peace. When the assault occurs in the context of war, it seems that additional dimensions of difficulty inhibit disclosure. This aspect is well-known in the research literature on sexual violence during wartime, as described above, and it is also significantly evident in the current context.

As stated, in our rape crisis centers, we estimate that in the coming years, some of those who have suffered sexual violence on October 7th and in the subsequent war may decide to share their stories.

Findings

First Analytical Axis: Arenas

Analysis of the data reveals that sexual and gender-based violence systematically occurred in all arenas where the October 7th massacre occurred, as well as in captivity. The following are the general outlines of the occurrences in each of the scenes, as they emerge.

The "Nova" Festival

The music festival "Nova" took place in an open area near Kibbutz Re'im, produced especially for the Sukkot holiday. It was held between October 6th and October 7th, hosting about 4,400 attendees.[7] At 6:22, sirens sounded in the festival area, and shortly after, it was decided to close the festival and disperse the celebrating crowd. Simultaneously, terrorists infiltrated the area with trucks and paragliders, seizing, assaulting, murdering, and taking attendees captive.

The crimes that occurred at the Festival area took place in the festival compound and at several sites in its vicinity, where participants fled attempting to escape the terrorists and missile fire. Some were captured in bomb shelters and hiding places where they tried to take refuge.

A day after the massacre, a video was posted on social media showing a woman in a torn dress, without underwear, injured and with her face burned. Police investigators estimated that she had been raped.[8] The woman who filmed the video (while searching for her friend, who was later found to have been kidnapped) recounted that a cut wound appeared on the body's leg, which she estimated was caused when her underwear was cut off.[9]

Several survivors of the massacre provided eyewitness testimony of gang rape, where women were abused and handled between multiple terrorists who beat, injured, and ultimately killed them.[10]

One survivor who wandered the area after the massacre described it as an "apocalypse of bodies, girls without clothes, some missing their upper, some their lower parts."[11]

These descriptions align with accounts from personnel who treated and removed the bodies, who testified about many bodies arriving partially clothed or unclothed, heavy bleeding from the pelvic area, and mutilation of genital organs.[12]

Kibbutzim and Villages in the South

During the October 7th attack, terrorists entered

homes in kibbutzim and villages in the western Negev. Due to the timing of the attack — the holiday of Simchat Torah — some of the homes hosted family members and guests who came for the holiday. The terrorists broke into hundreds of homes, murdered their inhabitants or took them captive by threatening them with weapons or by setting the homes on fire.

According to rescuers' testimonies and forensic evidence, signs of sexual assault were found in many homes near the murder scenes. In many cases, it appears that the acts were committed in the presence of spouses or other family members who were forced to witness the violence.

In Kibbutz Be'eri, where 90 of its residents were murdered, several testimonies were collected regarding the bodies of women and girls who were raped, mostly in their bedrooms, while partially dressed in their pajamas. ZAKA volunteers and rescue forces described a row of houses where bodies with signs of sexual assault were found, including women and girls who were stripped of their underwear,[13] signs of semen,[14] and insertion of a knife into the genital area.[15]

Similar testimonies were provided to the Association of Rape Crisis Centers by soldiers and rescue forces who evacuated bodies in other kibbutzim. Chaim Otmazgin, commander of the special units in ZAKA and an officer in the National Rescue and Fire Command, describes another kibbutz where he saw two naked bodies of women with objects penetrating their bodies.[16] Nira Shpak, a resident of Kfar Aza who took upon herself the task of identifying the bodies of the 60 killed in the kibbutz, recounted several bodies found with exposed intimate organs, sometimes with their clothes seemingly torn apart.[17]

Noam Mark, a member of the emergency security team

of Kibbutz Re'im, found three bodies of young women from the festival in one of the houses.[18] The bodies were found naked, with clear signs of severe sexual violence.[19] Mark provided the police with testimony along with a video supporting his claims.[20]

Research by *The New York Times* presents at least 24 bodies with signs of sexual abuse in Be'eri and Kfar Aza.[21] Additional information about sexual assaults on surviving young women, originally not disclosed, has reached the rape crisis centers.[22]

Israel Defense Force (IDF) Bases

Information about the incidents at IDF bases is relatively limited, but also includes gender-based and sexual assaults. Lieutenant Tamar Bar Shimon, who survived the invasion into the base at Erez Crossing, recounted how a terrorist threatened her with a weapon and demanded she remove her uniform.[23] She was rescued when another terrorist apprehended him.

Rescue personnel who attended to the bodies described those of female soldiers with signs of sexual violence. Shari Mendes, a volunteer who attended to women's bodies at the "Shura" camp,[24] reported seeing four bodies of female soldiers with signs of sexual violence, some with extensive bleeding in the pelvic area.[25] Maayan, a dentist and military officer who also worked at the camp, said she saw at least 10 bodies of female soldiers with clear signs of sexual violence.[26] Moshe Pinchi, an officer in the Israeli police, showed *The New York Times* a video featuring two soldiers who were shot in their genitals, which was filmed by Hamas operatives and retrieved by the IDF.[27]

Additional information about sexual assault of female soldiers, which was not initially disclosed, reached the rape crisis centers.[28]

In Captivity

Information about gender-based and sexual assaults that occurred during captivity began to accumulate with the return of hostages to Israel. Unlike incidents that occurred in other arenas, where many of the victims were murdered, these assaults were perpetrated against individuals who, hopefully, are still alive. Special sensitivity is required in dealing with these assaults, which concern the mental health of individuals who are still alive, and upon their release, will be entitled to choose whether and how to tell their stories.

Published testimonies indicate that both men and women were sexually assaulted during captivity.[29] Chen and Agam Goldstein, a mother and her teenage daughter who were kidnapped from their home in Kfar Aza and released after 51 days in captivity, noted that they encountered at least three female hostages who suffered sexual assault during captivity.[30]

Aviva Sigal, who was also kidnapped from her home in Kfar Aza and released after over 50 days in captivity, also spoke about sexual assaults on young women, including a case where she saw a young woman immediately after being assaulted when taken to the bathroom.[31]

She testified that Hamas militants turned both women and men into "puppets on a string."[32]

Second Analytical Axis: Mapping Patterns of Sexual Assault

Sexual assault during wartime is a phenomenon with

interrelated occurrences, rather than a collection of anecdotal cases. In this section, we will present an analysis of activity patterns — the patterns of abuse that recurred in the sexual and gender-based assaults committed during the events of October 7th and thereafter.

During the analysis of the testimonies and information at our disposal, both from open sources and classified ones, it emerged that the patterns can be divided into two main categories:

- War Rape Practices: Patterns of action used to perpetrate sexual assault during an armed conflict.
- Sadistic Practices: Practices characterized by brutal, demonstrative features aimed at intensifying the degradation and terror of sexual assault both physically and symbolically.

In most of the assaults, in addition to the first category of practices, practices from the second category were also prevalent.

The Practice of Rape During War

Systematic Use of Brutal Violence to Commit Rape

From various accounts, it emerges that during the raids on the kibbutzim, the capturing of civilians and soldiers (both women and men), and their captivity, Hamas militants systematically carried out acts of rape that involved penetrating the bodies of women, some of whom were injured, while employing brutal violence. Survivors of the Nova massacre who provided eyewitness testimonies of rape described rapes of injured women, or further injury during the rape, culminating in murder when finished.

Sapir, a survivor of the Nova massacre who provided detailed eyewitness testimony to the police, described how from a hiding place near Highway 232, she saw a large group of Hamas militants dressed in uniforms, passing injured women between them. She described five different rape cases she witnessed. In one instance, she saw a young woman with a back injury, her pants pulled down below her knees, being pulled by one terrorist by her hair while another terrorist was penetrating her. Each time the woman resisted, the terrorist stabbed her in the back. In another case, she saw how while one terrorist was raping a woman, another was cutting her and mutilating her body.[33]

Raz Cohen and Shoham Gueta, survivors from the festival who hid in another section of Highway 232, recounted seeing terrorists raping a young naked woman and stabbing her repeatedly. "Literally butchering her," according to Gueta.[34] In another interview given by Cohen, he testified that during the brutal rape, he saw that "the girl wasn't moving anymore. But the terrorist continued raping her."[35]

Yoni Saadon, a survivor from the festival who witnessed the rape of a young woman enduring severe violence, recounted hearing the victim screaming, "'Stop it — already I'm going to die anyway from what you are doing, just kill me!' When they finished they were laughing and the last one shot her in the head."[36]

Gad Liberson, who survived the festival, testified to hearing the abuse from his hiding place: "I hear shots, gunfire, bursts over our heads, and I hear girls speaking in English: 'Help,' 'No,' 'Please.' ... The girls were crying.

It sounded like they were being raped. They take them to the pickup trucks, they cry, they scream. They shoot them. I heard men's voices screaming, and when I heard shots they immediately stopped screaming. I heard the girls for a long time."[37]

Another survivor from the festival recounted in his testimony to police seeing bodies of women on the ground who were brutally raped. "There were girls there whose pelvises were simply broken from being raped so much."[38]

In addition, the rescuers who retrieved the bodies also described signs of rape alongside other severe injuries. These accounts were repeated about incidences in the vicinity of the festival[39] and in homes in the kibbutzim.[40]

Colonel Israel Weiss, who was involved in identifying bodies at the military rabbinate camp "Shura," testified that some of the bodies had undergone torture and rape.[41] Shari Mendes, who was involved in identifying female bodies at the camp, reported that acts of rape were directed at women of all ages, from children to the elderly, and were carried out so brutally that they led to fractures of their pelvic bones.[42]

Multiple Abusers/Gang Rape

From the various descriptions of the eyewitnesses, it appears that the sexual assaults and acts of rape were committed by several participants, as well as in the presence of other witnesses and excited crowds.

Sapir, a survivor of the Nova Festival, described the beginning of the acts of rape she witnessed at a sort of meeting point of dozens of men, most of them dressed in Hamas uniforms, who were passing weapons from hand to hand — and wounded women. She described several cases of rape that were committed in cooperation by multiple perpetrators. In another case of rape, "They bent someone over. I realized he was raping her and passing her on to someone else also in uniform."[43]

Raz Cohen and Shoham Gueta, survivors of the festival, reported that five (Cohen) or four (Gueta) terrorists participated in the rape they saw.[44] According to Yoni Saadon, between eight and ten terrorists participated in the rape case he witnessed.[45]

Rape in the Presence of Family/Community Members

In some cases, the sexual abuse took place in front of family members or friends who were forced to watch the sexual abuse under threat to the victim's life and their own, without the ability of acting to stop it.

This pattern emerged clearly in the testimonies of the ZAKA teams that collected and cleared kibbutz bodies, who found the bodies of women in the homes with signs of sexual abuse, alongside the bodies of family members or friends who seemed to have been forced to witness the abuse.

Chaim Otmazgin, of ZAKA and an officer in the search and rescue unit of the Home Front Command, told of a house where a mother's body was found with her hands cuffed behind her back with clear signs of struggle, while the body of her daughter (a girl or a young woman) was found in the next room with her pants and underwear rolled down.[46] Itzik Itach, a ZAKA volunteer, described a couple — man and woman — who were found tied to each other, naked, with clear signs of rape on the woman's body.[47] Nachman Dyksztejna, another volunteer, described the bodies of two women found tied by their hands and feet to a bed, one having been sexually abused and found with a knife in her genitals.[48]

An IDF paramedic described a room where the bodies of two girls were found, one of whom was found with her pants rolled down and the remains of semen on her back.[49] The Association of Rape Crisis Centers received additional information about soldiers who found the bodies of family members, with the woman's body without clothes and with signs of sexual abuse. According to the position of the body, it seems that her partner was forced to watch the sexual abuse before their murders.[50]

At the festival, it seems that the crowd present during the attack was mainly made up of festival-goers who were murdered (along with the witnesses who hid and gave testimony about what they saw and heard). Rami Davidian, a resident of the area who independently rescued hundreds of people from the festival, told the Association of Rape Crisis Centers that he found the bodies of "a boyfriend and girlfriend, they stripped them, (looks like) they were told to hug and they died hugging. There were beatings on their bodies. They abused them."[51] Also, festival-goers whose bodies with signs of abuse were found in Kibbutz Re'im were found together in the same space, in a way that shows that the abuse was committed together.[52]

The rape crisis centers received information about similar cases in which witnesses were forced to watch the abuse and survived.

Sexual Offenses of Males

From the evidence and information gathered, it

appears that sexual abuse was also committed against men.

According to the testimonies of the ZAKA members who collected the bodies from the festival area and the houses, some of the men who were found were also sexually abused. In some cases, their intimate organs were mutilated.[53] Chaim Otmazgin described the body of a man from the Festival that was stripped and shackled, and an attempt was made to burn him.[54]

A witness who was rescued from the Festival describes that she saw bodies of men whose genitals had been cut off.[55] A paramedic who described the injuries stated that the injuries were also to the men and that "There were a lot of gun wounds there. Shooting was targeted at sexual organs. We saw that a lot. They had a thing with sexual organs."[56]

Nirah Shpak from Kfar Aza testified that she saw the body of a man who was left naked from the waist down.[57]

Medical teams that treated the hostages who were released from captivity reported that men were also sexually assaulted in captivity.[58]

Execution During or After the Rape

Eyewitnesses to rape at the Nova Festival described cases in which the terrorists shot the victims in the head during the rape or immediately after.

According to Sapir, a survivor of the Nova Festival, in one case the rapist "shot her in the head while he was raping her, he didn't even pull up his pants."[59] Yoni Saadon described how "When they finished they were laughing and the last one shot her in the head."[60]

Another survivor of the Nova Festival provided the

police with earwitness testimony, which stated that after the rape, the terrorists set fire to the women. "We heard girls that were pulled out of the shelters, girls that shouted, they raped girls, burned them just after that. All the bodies outside were burned...."[61]

The video documenting the body of a woman who participated in the festival illustrates that after the assault, the body was burned.

Drawn from the fact that so many of the bodies were found with signs of sexual abuse, it paints a clear picture that after the assaults, they were killed.

Sadistic Practices

Binding and Tying

From the descriptions provided by the rescue and aid forces who arrived at the scenes of the massacre, it emerged that a significant portion of the bodies showing signs of sexual assault were found bound and gagged, and sometimes even tied to one another.

In fact, almost all testimonies about the presence of family members describe the binding of the sexual assault victim or the family member forced to witness the assault, as indicated by the testimonies of Itach,[62] Dyksztejna,[63] and Autmazgin.[64]

The New York Times interviewed four rescuers from the Nova Festival who described the sight of women's bodies with spread legs, without underwear, some with hands tied with ropes and zip ties. The bodies were found at the main area, but also along the road, in the park, and in open fields — places where the attendees fled in an attempt to save their lives. Jamal Waraki, a ZAKA volunteer, recounted a body of a young woman whose "hands were tied behind her back, she was bent forward, half-naked, her underwear stripped below her knees."[65]

Rescuer Rami Davidian said that he saw more than five bodies of women "tied to trees. Each one three, five meters from the other. Naked. They were tied with clothes or blankets around the tree with their hands, or standing leaning tied to the tree."[66]

Mutilation and Destruction of Genital Organs

From the testimonies of eyewitnesses, rescue, and medical forces, a picture emerges of deliberate harm to the genital organs of both men and women. This includes, among other things, direct and targeted shooting, mutilation of organs, and destruction and burning of sexual and intimate organs.

Shari Mendes, who worked on the "Shura" base identifying bodies, describes that a large number of bodies arrived with gunshot wounds to the genitals and chest, alongside systematic mutilation of sexual organs.[67]

Bodies of women were found with gunshot wounds targeted at the breasts and genital mutilation, some with severed breasts. Mendes described it as "this seemed to be a systematic genital mutilation of a group of victims."[68]

ZAKA personnel reported finding naked, injured women with mutilated sexual organs.[69] Chaim Otmazgin from ZAKA added that many of the bodies were found partially clothed or unclothed, with severe bleeding from the pelvis and destruction of sexual organs, indicating that even when there was no time to complete the rape, there was an intentional attempt to destroy the sexual organs to harm the "dignity" of the woman.[70]

Sapir's eyewitness testimony about the rapes at Nova include description of breast amputation with a box cutter. After the breast was cut off, Sapir describes how the terrorists threw it on the floor and passed it between them like a toy.[71]

Yinon Rivlin, who also survived the Nova Festival, described how at one point he left his hiding place to search for more survivors. Next to the road, he saw the body of a young woman lying on her stomach, without pants or underwear, her legs spread. Her genitalia seemed "as if someone tore her apart."[72]

Rami Davidian told ARCCI that the bodies of women tied to trees also had "mutilation in intimate places that is hard to see... all their organs were cut, damaged. Blood from the genitals. They inserted iron rods into their sexual organs... there were shots in the breasts."[73]

Bodies of men were found with their genitalia severed, while others had their genitalia shot and mutilated. According to testimonies from ZAKA personnel, the intimate organs of men who suffered sexual assault were mutilated.[74] The police presented testimony from a survivor of the Nova Festival, who also described bodies of men with severed genitalia.[75] Also Mendes, who dealt with bodies in "Shura," described harm to the genitalia of men.[76] Davidian recounted seeing the body of a man directly shot in the genitalia.[77]

Insertion of Weapons in Intimate Areas

Another form of assault included the insertion of weapons into genital organs — nails, grenades, and knives. It represents a specific expression of the pattern of targeted mutilation and harm to sexual organs.

ZAKA volunteer Nachman Dyksztejna described that in Be'eri, he saw the body of a woman with a knife inserted in her genital organ.[78]

Mendes reported that "occasionally there was a need to evacuate the base because some of the victims arrived booby-trapped."[79]

Chaim Otmazgin from ZAKA described finding a naked body with a sharp object stuck in her genitalia, and another with an object penetrated through her anus. In a conversation we had with him, he described how he saw "a woman's body stabbed in the genitalia with a serrated knife that was used to remove the woman's internal organs, leaving them between her legs."[80]

Simcha Greenman, another ZAKA volunteer, testified that he saw in one of the houses the body of a woman with sharp objects stuck in her genitals, including nails.[81]

The New York Times reported that they saw a picture of a woman's body with dozens of nails embedded in her knees and pelvis.[82]

Destruction and Mutilation of the Body

In many cases, alongside the sexual assault, deliberate mutilation of the body occurred, including facial mutilation, burning, decapitation, and disfigurement. Many bodies were found with detached heads, making the identification and burial of the victims more difficult.

Sapir, a survivor of the Nova Festival, describes a rape incident in which the terrorists cut off the victim's breasts, followed by cutting her face. With the disfigurement of her face, she collapsed and fell out of Sapir's sight.[83]

Chaim Otmazgin from ZAKA describes the body of

"a woman stripped of her clothes from the upper half of her body, they shot her in the head, and then they slaughtered her. The head was detached from the body. They didn't come to kill, they came to mutilate."[84] In an interview he gave, he recounted that the sight of the mutilated bodies repeated itself at the festival scene. One of the festival participants, he says, had their chest cut open. "It's not easy to cut a body. This is someone who did it and didn't stop. [...] There's almost no body they were satisfied with [just] shooting."[85]

Summary

From the testimonies and information provided, it emerges that the sexual assaults committed during the October 7th attack and thereafter were carried out systematically and deliberately. Sexual assaults took place (and may still be ongoing) in all areas of the attack, as described: the Nova Festival, kibbutzim and villages in the south, IDF bases, and the captivity where children, women, and men kidnapped on October 7th were held, and some still are.

From accounts of the atrocities, it appears that the perpetrators' actions match patterns of wartime sexual violence documented in literature; practices that describe rape and gender-based violence often appear in combination with sadistic practices with demonstratively brutal characteristics.

Some of the cases described by witnesses were carried out by multiple perpetrators, sometimes with others aiding, encouraging, or perpetrating additional assaults, such as stabbing or shooting. Thus, the victim is effectively under a double attack: sexual assault and armed assault simultaneously. Literature estimates that about 90% of wartime rape cases are committed by multiple perpetrators.[86] According to literature, gang rape is intended to prove masculinity to others[87] and to meet the social expectations of the other fighters/perpetrators present.[88]

In addition, it appears that instances of sexual assault occurred in front of audiences including family members, community members, or other relatives. This practice is known in literature and aims to undermine the dignity and masculinity of men who fail to protect their women,[89] as well as to instill fear to deepen oppression and degradation. When other women are forced to witness the sexual assault, even if they were not themselves victims, they are influenced and subdued by the perpetrator's power.[90] Forcing spouses, parents, and siblings to witness the sexual assault of a family member is a practice of torture. In many cases, family members are killed when they try to protect their family from sexual assault.[91]

From the testimonies of the attacks at the Festival, it appears that the terrorists sought and captured women who tried to escape; some hid but were caught. A "hunt" for captured women is also known in literature, where intruders find a hiding woman and then assault her in full view.[92] Also dragging women by their hair while they scream, after being captured, as described by various witnesses who survived the Festival, is a way to sow fear, harm the community, and establish control over the enemy through psychological and physical means.[93]

Evidence of the events of October 7th show that children and men were also assaulted. However, information about this phenomenon is relatively scarce at this stage and focuses on body mutilation. The limited exposure of sexual assaults on men, even in comparison to the limited exposure of sexual assaults in war, is considered characteristic of the phenomenon. Generally, men suffer from compounded shame when disclosing sexual assaults, which are perceived as deeply humiliating and an attack on masculinity. They are reported at much lower rates. It is reasonable to assume that male survivors in this case will have more difficulty seeking help. Rescue forces may have also refrained from describing such "embarrassing" injuries.

Evidence of tying and binding bodies, likely performed during the assaults, sometimes to other family members, is a practice of humiliation and exertion of power, as well as harming and using others.

The brutal practices of mutilating intimate organs of girls, women, and men, as well as cutting of women's breasts, are intended to signify permanent injury and further destruction in addition to the sexual assault.[94] According to field rescuers, the mutilation of genital organs is intended to reinforce the victim's own degradation and symbolically, also that of the state that failed to protect them.

It is worth noting that according to reports, Iranian forces also engage in practices of targeted disfigurement of detained women's faces alongside committing acts of rape.[95]

Furthermore, the use of various weapons such as knives inserted into vaginas or hiding grenades in bodies is well-known in literature as an additional form of violence in sexual assaults,[96] as well as using them to threaten and coerce the victims.[97] This may be intended to convey a symbolic message of the perpetrator's overwhelming power and ability to reach anywhere.

In literature, wartime rape often appears with practices of sadism, xenophobia, and dehumanization. The practices described in this document illustrate the brutality and sadism characteristic of the way the assaults were carried out. Amputating genital organs, decapitation, and "playing" with women's breasts are particularly sadistic and violent practices performed in the presence and participation of other perpetrators.

During wartime, victims are dehumanized, with the violated woman or man not seen as human beings but rather as a symbolic body of the "enemy" onto which hatred and violence are projected.

The brutality is also evident in the physical injuries accompanying the sexual assault — for example, the amputation of organs, shooting, and the mutilation described, which constitutes a long-term harm that reaches the teams handling the bodies hours after they were captured and assaulted.

The systematic sexual assaults perpetrated by Hamas terrorists on October 7th mark a particularly painful milestone in the history of Israeli society. We, at the rape crisis centers for victims of sexual assault, understand well the heavy burden on many fronts: the survivors who have endured, first and foremost; family members and friends who were forced to witness their loved ones undergoing sexual abuse; eyewitnesses and audio witnesses; rescue, relief, and burial preparation teams who dealt with the bodies, carrying the burden with them; family members whose loved ones were abducted; the kidnapped and released hostages, some of whom "luckily" escaped rape, spoke of the intense anxiety beneath the ground and constant fear of rape; survivors of former sexual abuse who are in regular contact with the rape crisis centers and are suffering distress, psychological deterioration, and even suicidal thoughts with exposure to stories of trauma; and the entire Israeli society, within which something has been broken.

These days, as the scar in our hearts refuses to heal, and the souls of our sisters and brothers cry out to us from the ground, many of those we thought were partners and allies remain silent and therefore deny the horrors. We urge you to amplify their voices and not allow these victims to be silenced.

Endnotes

1. Hagen, K. & Yohani, S. (2010). The nature and psychosocial consequences of war rape for individuals and communities. *International journal of psychological studies*, 2(2), 14–25; Kerstiens, F. (2004). War rape: The aftermath for women. Unpublished master's thesis, Royal Roads University, Victoria, British Columbia, Canada.

2. Vlachova, M., & Biason, L. (Eds.). (2005). Women in an insecure world: Violence against women, facts, figures, and analysis. Geneva, Switzerland: Geneva Centre for the Democratic Control of Armed Forces.

3. Toole, M. J., & Waldman, R. J. (1997). The public health aspects of complex emergencies and refugee situations. Annual review of public health, 18(1), 283–312.

4. Hagen & Yohani, 2010.

5. Bernard, V., & Durham, H. (2014). Sexual violence in armed conflict: From breaking the silence to breaking the cycle. International Review of the Red Cross, 96(894), 427–434.

6. Hagen & Yohani, 2010.

7. Korial, A., Levi, L., & Glickman, A. (November 23, 2019). "Please, I'm begging. They're killing me": Investigation and tales of heroism from the massacre at Re'im. Ynet. www.ynet.co.il/news/article/yokra13681367 [Hebrew].

8. Gettelmanm, J., Schwartz, A., & Sella, A. (28.12.23). "Screams without words": How Hamas weaponized sexual violence on Oct. 7. *The New York Times*. www.nytimes.com/2023/12/28/world/middleeast/oct-7-attacks-hamas-israel-sexual-violence.html.

9. A conversation of the Association of Rape Crisis Centers with Eden Vasli, 31.1.23.

10. Lamb, C. (2.12.23). First Hamas fighters raped her. Then they shot her in the head. *The Sunday Times*. www.thetimes.co.uk/article/ten-hamas-fighters-were-raping-the-woman-she-begged-for-death-6ldlmh8sp *The Jewish Chronicle*; (3.12.23) Hamas gang raped and beheaded women at rave massacre, fresh testimony reveals. *The Jewish Chronicle*. www.thejc.com/news/israel/hamas-gang-raped-and-beheaded-women-at-rave-massacre-fresh-testimony-reveals-blp0ghdl; Gettelmanm, Schwartz, & Sella, 28.12.23.

11. Saban, A.(28.11.23). "More than 1,500 Harrowing Testimonies That the Mind and Soul Struggle to Digest": A Stirring Debate in the Committee for the Advancement of Women's Status. *Israel Hayom*. www.israelhayom.co.il/news/local/article/14879357 [Hebrew].

12. *Sky News* (1.2.24). Israel-Hamas war: Some female victims of 7 October 'had their faces obliterated.' *World News | Sky News*; Gettelmanm, Schwartz & Sella, 28.12.23.

13. A conversation of the Association of Rape Crisis Centers with Chaim Otmazgin, 28.1.24; Rose, E., & Villarraga, H. (17.10.23). Rescue workers recount horrors found in kibbutz attacked by Hamas. *Reuters*, www.reuters.com/world/middle-east/rescue-workers-recount-horrors-found-kibbutz-attacked-by-hamas-2023-10-17/; Keller-Lynn, C. (9.11.23). Amid war and urgent need to ID bodies, evidence of Hamas's October 7 rapes slips away. *The Times of Israel*. www.timesofisrael.com/amid-war-and-urgent-need-to-id-bodies-evidence-of-hamass-october-7-rapes-slips-away/.

14. Tapper. J. (16.11.23). 'Not just killed, cruelly mutilated': Witness describes assault of women on Oct. 7. *CNN* /edition.cnn.com/videos/world/2023/11/16/sexual-violence-israeli-women-hamas-attack-tapper-pkg-lead-vpx.cnn.

15. Williamson, L. (5.12.23). Israel Gaza: Hamas raped and mutilated women on 7 October, BBC hears. *BBC*. www.bbc.com/news/world-middle-east-67629181.

16. A conversation of the Association of Rape Crisis Centers with Chaim Otmazgin, 28.1.24.

17. A conversation of the Association of Rape Crisis Centers with Nira Shpak, 10.2.23.

18. It is unclear how the young women arrived at the kibbutz — whether they fled and tried to find refuge there, or whether they were brought in by the terrorists. In a conversation with

him, Mark estimates that it is the second possibility, as according to him, it was impossible to enter the kibbutz during the attack.

19. A conversation of the Association of Rape Crisis Centers with Noam Mark, 5.2.24.

20. Dadon, A. (30.12.23). First publication The unpublished eyewitness testimony to the acts of rape by Hamas terrorists on 7.10. *12 News.* www.mako.co.il/news-military/6361323d-dea5a810/Article-c18ee2771bbbc81026.htm [Hebrew].

21. Gettelmanm, Schwartz, & Sella, 28.12.23.

22. Confidential information received by the Association of Rape Crisis Centers.

23. Zaitoun. Y. (23.10.17). "Chilling testimony from a female officer who survived an ambush: "The terrorist wanted me to take off my uniform." *Ynet.* www.ynet.co.il/blogs/gazawar11/article/hy3deuhwp [Hebrew]; McKernan, B. (10.11.23). Israel women's groups warn of failure to keep evidence of sexual violence in Hamas attacks. *The Guardian.* www.theguardian.com/world/2023/nov/10/israel-womens-groups-warn-of-failure-to-keep-evidence-of-sexual-violence-in-hamas-attacks.

24. A military base where body identification took place for Israel, following the October 7th massacre.

25. Gettelmanm, Schwartz, & Sella, 28.12.23.

26. Keller-Lynn, 9.11.23.

27. Gettelmanm, Schwartz, & Sella, 28.12.23.

28. Classified information reached the ARCCI.

29. *The Times of Israel* (6.12.23). "At least 10 freed hostages were sexually abused in Hamas captivity, doctor says." www.timesofisrael.com/at-least-10-freed-hostages-were-sexually-abused-by-hamas-in-captivity-doctor-says/.

30. Perez. E. (11.12.23). Chen Goldstein-Almog who was released from captivity: three abductees told us that they were sexually assaulted, *Kan Resher Bet,* www.kan.org.il/content/kan-news/defense/650523/ [Hebrew]; *Ynet* (16.11.24), "When we were left alone, they told us they were sexually assaulted — and we cried": Agam, who left Gaza, fears being kidnapped.

www.ynet.co.il/news/article/skum8axta [Hebrew]; Shimoni, R. (11.12.23). They were held captive by Hamas, but their biggest fear was Israeli airstrikes. *Haaretz*. www.haaretz.com/israel-news/2023-12-11/ty-article-magazine/.premium/they-were-held-captive-by-hamas-but-their-biggest-fear-was-israeli-airstrikes/0000018c-554b-db23-ad9f-7ddb3c990000.

31. Aharon, D. (9.1.2024). Rape and torture in captivity: The harrowing testimony of the released captive. *Kan*, www.kan.org.il/content/kan-news/local/681088/ [Hebrew].

32. Pelman, V. (23.1.23). Women released from captivity: "There are girls there who haven't had their period for a long time." *Kan*, www.kan.org.il/content/kan-news/local/690304/ [Hebrew].

33. Gettelmanm, Schwartz, & Sella, 28.12.23; Breiner, J. (8.11.23). Israeli police collect eyewitness testimony of gang rape during Hamas attack. *Haaretz* www.haaretz.com/israel-news/2023-11-08/ty-article/israeli-police-collect-eyewitness-testimony-of-gang-rape-during-hamas-attack/0000018b-b025-d3c1-a39b-bee5ef400000.

34. Gettelmanm, Schwartz, & Sella, 28.12.23.

35. *Kan Zman Emet* (14.12.23). "I saw and couldn't do anything:" testimonies of rape from the festival. www.kan.org.il/content/kan/kan-11/p-12043/s7/655396 [Hebrew].

36. *The Jewish Chronicle*, 3.12.23.

37. *Kan Zman Emet*, 14.12.23.

38. Saban, 28.11.23.

39. Eli, E. (November 14, 2023). "Flying with the pick-up truck from end to end": The farmer who rescued 120 young people from the festival in Re'im. *13 News*. 13tv.co.il/item/news/politics/security/hp8ai-903804236/.

40. E. Rose & H. Villarraga (17.10.23). Rescue workers recount horrors found in kibbutz attacked by Hamas. *Reuters*, www.reuters.com/world/middle-east/rescue-workers-recount-horrors-found-kibbutz-attacked-by-hamas-2023-10-17/.

41. *Reuters* (15.10.23) Israeli forensic teams describe signs of torture, abuse. www.reuters.com/world/middle-east/israeli-forensic-teams-describe-signs-torture-abuse-2023-10-15.

42. Visegrád 24. (24.10.23). An Israeli woman responsible for identifying female victims of the Hamas massacre confirms that Hamas terrorists raped children and elderly women. twitter.com/visegrad24/status/1716737563749237030.

43. Shimoni, 11.12.23.

44. Gettelmanm, Schwartz, & Sella, 28.12.23.

45. *The Jewish Chronicle*, 3.12.23.

46. A conversation of the Association of Rape Crisis Centers with Chaim Otmazgin, 28.1.24.

47. Rose & Villarraga, 17.10.23 Williamson, L. (5.12.23). Israel Gaza: Hamas raped and mutilated women on 7 October, BBC hears. BBC News. www.bbc.com/news/world-middle-east-67629181.

48. Williamson, 5.12.23.

49. Tapper, 17.11.23.

50. A conversation of the Association of Rape Crisis Centers with an IFD official, 31.10.23.

51. A conversation of the Association of Rape Crisis Centers with Rami Davidian, 7.2.24.

52. A conversation of the Association of Rape Crisis Centers with Noam Mark, 5.2.24.

53. Saban, A. (8.11.23). "She was raped and executed:" New evidence from the horrors of October 7 is revealed. *Israel Hayom* www.israelhayom.co.il/news/defense/article/14801490 [Hebrew].

54. A conversation of the Association of Rape Crisis Centers with Chaim Otmazgin, 28.1.23.

55. Saban, 28.11.23.

56. United Nations Event, 4.12.23, 41:30.

57. A conversation of the Association of Rape Crisis Centers with Nirah Shpak, 11.2.24.

58. *The Times of Israel*, 6.12.23.

59. Breiner, J. (8.11.2023) X. twitter.com/JoshBreiner/status/1722282840824614947?s=20.

60. *The Jewish Chronicle*, 3.12.23.

61. United Nations, 4.12.23, 41:30.

62. Rose & Villarraga, 17.10.23.

63. Williamson, 5.12.23.

64. A conversation of the Association of Rape Crisis Centers with Chaim Otmazgin, 28.1.24.

65. Williamson, 5.12.23.

66. A conversation of the Association of Rape Crisis Centers with Rami Davidian, 7.2.23.

67. United Nations, 4.12.23, 41:30.

68. ibid.

69. *Kan, Zman Emet*, 14.12.23.

70. A conversation of the Association of Rape Crisis Centers with Rami Davidian, 7.2.23.

71. Gettelmanm, Schwartz, & Sella, 28.12.23.

72. ibid.

73. A conversation of the Association of Rape Crisis Centers with Rami Davidian, 7.2.23.

74. Saban, 8.11.23.

75. Saban, 28.11.23.

76. United Nations, 4.12.23, 41:30.

77. A conversation of the Association of Rape Crisis Centers with Rami Davidian, 7.2.23.

78. Williamson, 5.12.23.

79. *Maariv*. (February 1, 2024). "Some of the victims arrived 'trapped'": New horrifying testimonies from Hamas atrocities exposed. www.maariv.co.il/news/world/Article-1072808 [Hebrew].

80. A conversation of the Association of Rape Crisis Centers with Chaim Otmazgin, 28.1.24.

81. McKernan, 10.11.23.

82. Gettelmanm, Schwartz, & Sella, 28.12.23.

83. ibid.

84. A conversation of the Association of Rape Crisis Centers with Chaim Otmazgin, 28.1.24.

85. *Kan, Zman Emet,* 14.12.23.

86. Vlachova & Biason, 2005.

87. Brownmiller, S. (1975). *Against our will: Men, women and rape.* New York: Simon and Schuster.

88. Hagen & Yohani, 2010.

89. Brownmiller, 1975.

90. Hagen & Yohani, 2010.

91. Chang, I. (1997). *The rape of Nanking: The forgotten holocaust of World War II.* New York: Basic Books.

92. Tompkins, T. (1995). Prosecuting rape as a war crime: Speaking the unspeakable. *Notre Dame Law Review.* 70(4), 845–890.

93. Schiessl, C. (2002). An element of genocide: rape, total war, and international law in the twentieth century. *Journal of Genocide Research,* 4(2), 197-210.

94. Amnesty International. (2004). Violence against women fire in war-torn countries. www.amnesty.org/fr/wp-content/uploads/2021/06/nws210102004en.pdf; Vlachova & Biason, 2005.

95. Razavi, E. (13.6.23). KURDISTAN DES GUERRI RES CONTRE LES MOLLAHS. Paris. www.parismatch.com/actu/international/kurdistan-des-guerrieres-contre-les-mollahs-226175.

96. Bop, C. (2001). Women in conflicts, their gains and their losses. In S. Meintjes, A. Pillay, & M. Turshen (Eds.), *The aftermath: Women in post-conflict transformation* (pp. 19-33). New York: Zed Books; Kerstiens, 2004.

97. Hagen & Yohani, 2010.

Male October 7 Survivor Recounts Rape at Hands of Hamas Terrorists

Times of Israel Staff (24/07/2024)

A SURVIVOR OF THE Hamas massacre at the Supernova music festival on October 7 said he was raped by terrorists attacking the rave, the first time a male victim has come forward to publicly detail sexual offenses during the brutal assault.

The testimony by the victim, whose comments to Channel 12 News were aired without revealing his identity, add to a growing body of evidence that terrorists who stormed into Israel on October 7 sexually assaulted their victims, both male and female.

Firsthand testimony of such acts has been fairly rare, as most of the victims were killed, a fact that some Israel critics have used to sow doubts about the allegations.

The victim was with hundreds others fleeing terrorists who descended upon the festival near Kibbutz Re'im early on October 7, when he said he was caught by forces from Hamas's elite Nukhba unit.

"They pin you to the ground, you try to resist, they take off your clothes, laugh at you, humiliate you, spit at you," he said, his face blurred and his voice distorted to avoid recognition. "They touched [private] parts, they rape you."

"There is a circle, [people] laugh, and you don't know what to do in the moment, whether you should resist or let it pass, how to deal with the situation. There was a very difficult rape. At some point more people arrived and called for them and so they had to stop," added the man, who was identified by the Hebrew initial Dalet.

"It's a very tough moment. Weakness in the entire body. As if your blood is cheap. They were wildly intoxicated, celebrating, laughing with their pistols, with their knives. You disassociate yourself from the situation, but on the other hand experience it very strongly. Very difficult," he said.

Dalet eventually managed to escape, the report said, with the help of Israeli forces that showed up.

Asked how he has been coping with the experience, Dalet replied, "It wasn't simple in the beginning. I was very closed off." He also reported an obsessive fixation on cleanliness in the aftermath of the attack. "A lot, a lot of showers, to get all that energy off me, everything that happened."

Dalet's testimony has been handed to a police unit investigating sexual crimes committed by the terrorists on October 7, after he filed a complaint, the report said.

Aware that some are casting doubt on testimony of sexual violence on October 7, Dalet has presented various sources with medical opinions that testify to the harm done to him, as well as sitting for a polygraph test.

His testimony is also included in a major lawsuit filed by more than 100 survivors of the Supernova festival against the State of Israel, demanding more than NIS 500 million ($137 million) in government support.

"Many of them aren't able to return to work, and aren't

able to return to their lives — to address [the case of] Dalet specifically, of course it's impossible, at this stage, to return to normal life after what happened," said Einat Ginzburg, one of the lawyers representing the massacre survivors.

Israeli police have been collecting survivor testimony, physical evidence, and confessions of sexual assault by terrorists on October 7 since the immediate aftermath of the attack, when thousands of terrorists burst into southern Israel from the Gaza Strip, killing some 1,200 people and taking 251 hostages, starting the ongoing war.

A February report by the United Nations Secretary-General on Sexual Violence in Conflict found that "there are reasonable grounds to believe that conflict-related sexual violence occurred during the 7 October attacks in multiple locations across the Gaza periphery, including rape and gang rape, in at least three locations."

The report also testified to "clear and convincing" evidence that hostages were raped while being held in Gaza, and that those currently held captive are still facing such abuse.

Further evidence was made public in April by the release of a one-hour documentary on the topic directed by former Meta CEO Sheryl Sandberg, called *Screams Before Silence*, which is free to watch online.

Amit Soussana, an Israeli hostage who was released during a weeklong truce in November, was the first to speak publicly about being sexually abused in captivity, recounting being marched at gunpoint to the bedroom of her captor, where he forced her to "commit a sexual act on him."

Teenager Agam Goldstein-Almog, also released in the November deal, reported having been groped by captors and being constantly afraid she would be raped. "Half of the girls and young women I met in captivity told me they experienced sexual or physical abuse or both. They are still living there with their rapists," she said at the time.

Unmasking the Horrors: Hamas's Weaponization of Sexual Violence — Summarizing the Facts

Moshe Kaplan, MD

WHEN HAMAS LAUNCHED its brutal and unprecedented attack on Israel on October 7th, 2023, it resulted in widespread physical, sexual, and emotional abuse against both civilians and hostages. The attacks on Israeli communities, in which Hamas killed 1,139 people and kidnapped 240 hostages into Gaza, involved widespread sexual violence. Detailed testimonies and forensic evidence have revealed the extent of these atrocities, both during the initial assault and in the subsequent captivity of hostages. Despite the overwhelming proof, global recognition of these crimes has been disturbingly slow, overshadowed by criticism of Israel and outright denials by Hamas.

During the Hamas-led attack, Hamas or other Gazan militants subjected Israeli women and girls to sexual violence, including rape and sexual assault. Various sources have extensively documented these acts of gender-based violence, war crimes, and crimes against humanity, although Hamas has consistently denied that its fighters committed rape and assault against women.

Testimonies from released hostages indicated that both female and male captives experienced sexual violence while Hamas held them in Gaza. In late March 2024, Amit Soussana became the first Israeli hostage to publicly state that she was sexually abused while Hamas followers held her captive.

A UN report in March 2024 concluded there was "clear and convincing information" that Israeli hostages in Gaza experienced "sexual violence, including rape." The report also found "reasonable grounds" to believe such abuse was ongoing. This report, while not investigative in nature, aimed to collect and confirm allegations, noting that a "fully fledged" investigation would be needed to establish definitive proof.

Israel Defense Forces and Israeli officials have provided evidence suggesting that hundreds of Israeli women were raped, sexually abused, or mutilated. Hamas fighters infiltrated Israeli towns, where witnesses reported that they tortured, raped, and sexually assaulted hundreds of women and girls, and some men. For example, a paramedic from the 669 Special Tactics Rescue Unit in Kibbutz Be'eri found the bodies of two teenage girls in a bedroom, one of whom had been raped. Other accounts from survivors and first responders detailed instances of gang rape, mutilation, and severe physical abuse. Tel Aviv University professor Tamar Herzig reported that militants discussed plans to rape specific girls and paraded victims with their clothes ripped off and blood between their legs.

Despite these horrific accounts, the global response has been muted. It wasn't until December that the UN

Women agency condemned Hamas's gender-based violence. Israeli feminist organizations and public figures have criticized this delay and the silence of global feminist organizations, especially given the severity and scale of the crimes.

Hamas has denied committing these atrocities, citing Islamic teachings that forbid such acts. However, numerous reports and testimonies contradict these denials. Israeli security agencies collected extensive evidence, including video footage and photographs of victims' bodies, confirming the accounts of sexual assault. Autopsies of victims corroborated these reports, revealing signs of rape, genital mutilation, and severe trauma.

The international community has responded with a troubling denial of these atrocities. For example, Basem Naim, a Hamas spokesperson, dismissed Soussana's testimony as potentially fabricated, despite the overwhelming evidence. This denial hinders efforts to hold perpetrators accountable and provide justice for the victims.

The atrocities were not limited to the initial attacks but continued in captivity. Survivors like Maya Regev recounted continuous sexual harassment and assault by their captors. Released hostages underwent pregnancy tests and screenings for sexually transmitted diseases, further indicating the extent of the sexual abuse they endured.

The stories of physical, sexual, and emotional abuse inflicted by Hamas since October 7th present a clear and harrowing picture of its brutality. These accounts highlight the urgent need for international recognition and condemnation of these crimes. The survivors' courage in sharing their experiences should serve as a powerful reminder of the horrors they endured and the need for justice and accountability.

The silence and slow response from global organizations, coupled with biased narratives that downplay or deny the suffering of Israeli victims, only add to the victims' trauma. It is imperative that the world hear these voices and acknowledge these stories in order to ensure that such horrors are never repeated. The world must stand with the victims, condemn the perpetrators, and work tirelessly to bring justice to those who have suffered at the hands of Hamas.

The atrocities that Hamas committed on October 7th have left an indelible mark on the survivors and the broader global community. In the face of the overwhelming evidence, the world has slowly come to terms with the depth of physical, sexual, and emotional abuse that Hamas inflicted on Israeli civilians and hostages. Here, we delve into detailed reports and testimonies that shed light on these heinous acts and the response they have elicited.

In February 2024, the Association of Rape Crisis Centers in Israel (ARCCI) published a comprehensive 35-page report detailing the extent of sexual violence that Hamas carried out during the October 7th attacks. The findings, partly based on statements from ZAKA members, revealed that these assaults were more widespread than initially understood. The report emphasized that rapes often occurred in the presence of an audience, including partners, family members, or friends, amplifying the pain, humiliation, and trauma for all involved. It concluded that there was clear evidence of "systematic, targeted sexual abuse" of women during the Hamas-led assault on southern Israel.

Adding to this, a December 2023 *New York Times* investigation entitled, "Screams Without Words: How Hamas

Weaponized Sexual Violence on Oct. 7" provided a detailed account of the rape and sexual violence during the attack. The article described the way that Hamas systematically used sexual violence as a weapon of war. Despite facing criticism for relying heavily on witness testimony and lacking some forensic evidence, *The Times* stood by its report, asserting that it was rigorously sourced and edited.

Survivors from the Nova Music Festival also shared their traumatic experiences. Raz Cohen witnessed terrorists laughing as they raped and murdered a woman. The attackers treated the violence as entertainment, underscoring the extreme sexual violence and utter disregard for human life that the Hamas fighters exhibited. Similar stories emerged from other locations, such as Kibbutz Be'eri, where a paramedic found the bodies of two teenage girls who had been raped and murdered.

Despite these detailed accounts and corroborating evidence, the global response has been disappointingly slow. Feminist organizations and international bodies, which should have been vocal in condemning such gender-based violence, have often remained silent. It wasn't until December that the UN Women's agency condemned Hamas's gender-based violence, a delay that has been widely criticized.

The fact of these crimes is undeniable. Israeli police and military collected extensive forensic evidence, including video footage and photographs of victims' bodies, which confirmed accounts of sexual assault. Autopsies revealed that many women had been raped, mutilated, and murdered, often in front of witnesses or family members.

These reports and testimonies paint a clear and

harrowing picture of the brutality that Hamas has inflicted since October 7th. The courage of survivors in sharing their experiences should serve as a powerful reminder of the horrors they endured and the need for justice and accountability. It is imperative that the international community recognize and condemn these atrocities unequivocally, stand with the victims, and hold the perpetrators accountable for their heinous actions.

The aftermath of these barbaric acts is the manifestation of Jewish resilience.

> *"Instead of fighting the darkness, bring in the light."* — Eckhart Tolle

Chapter Five

Resilience

*"It's your reaction to adversity,
not adversity itself, that determines how
your life story will develop."*
–Dieter Uchtdorf

Everything Is a Miracle

Moshe Kaplan, MD

NONE OTHER THAN Albert Einstein said, "Either everything is a miracle or nothing is a miracle." Certainly one of the greatest miracles of all time is the survival of the Jewish people — having survived pogroms, inquisitions, blood libels, massacres, the Holocaust and more — and our resilience continues.

Israeli women have shown resilience from Day One, as Dr. Miriam Adelson noted: "One dramatic achievement has been clear from the very first minutes of October 7. The women of Israel have earned their reward for the blood, sweat, and tears their sisters shed for the whole nation and all of humanity. Demonstrating their resilience, women became engaged in frontline combat against the enemy. Hamas is discovering, to its misfortune, that women will be the victors in this war. The fact that slender fingers with painted nails press the button that sends many of the terrorists to hell creates a special sense of humiliation for those who preach male supremacy."

We have a tremendous capacity for finding the resilience that allows us to endure difficulties when we believe they are providing purpose to our lives. Our resilience will help us to overcome. The programs that this chapter presents, as well as many others, do exactly that.

Unyielding Resilience —
The Jewish Spirit from Ancient Trials to Modern Heroism

Moshe Kaplan, MD

IN TIMES OF adversity and persecution, the Jewish people have demonstrated a remarkable ability to rise, stronger and more resilient than before. This concept is known as anti-fragility — the spiritual alchemy of turning pain into purpose.

This resilience is a recurring theme throughout Jewish history, exemplified during significant events such as Passover, when the Jewish people endured and overcame prolonged persecution and hardship in Egypt. Over approximately 200 years, a small group of 70 souls who entered Egypt became enslaved, but ultimately left as a nation three million strong, ready to receive the Torah at Mount Sinai. One of the most harrowing periods during this enslavement was the genocidal decree of Pharaoh, who ordered the murder of the firstborn male infants. Despite his efforts to decimate them and destroy their will, the Jewish people not only survived but thrived, as the Torah states, "The more they oppressed them, the more they increased" (Exodus 1:11).

This spirit of resilience has continued throughout

Jewish history, turning major setbacks into opportunities for extraordinary new adventures in Jewish spirit and creativity. The same heroism that motivated Jews to overcome despair and terror during the Holocaust occurred on October 7. Minister Benny Gantz reflected on the fact that "our enemies sought to destroy, intimidate, and break us up, yet found us more united and determined." At a Holocaust Memorial Day commemoration at the Massuah International Institute for Holocaust Studies, Gantz spoke about the incredible courage that people displayed during the Holocaust. Despite facing the evil forces of the Nazis, hunger, loss, and the smell of death from the ovens, the Jewish people held on to the strength of their souls.

Gantz recounted stories of children who jumped from trains and ran under barrages of fire to freedom, adults who shared their last slice of bread despite their own hunger, and heroes who survived, fought, and later came to Israel to continue fighting for the resurrection of their people. These stories of heroism reverberated in the days following October 7. Gantz shared his conversations with hundreds who had gone through hell, noting that he had heard the phrase "second Holocaust" over and over. These were stories of little children who lay in shelters, conquering their fear; those of soldiers, police officers, members of the security and rescue forces; and civilians who fought battles with resourcefulness and courage. Many rescued hundreds under fire. Young people jumped on grenades in shelters and fought terrorists with their bare hands, demonstrating a profound sense of mutual responsibility and sacrifice.

The Jewish people's resilience is a testament to their ability to transform suffering into strength, continuing to thrive despite the gravest of challenges. From the trials in Egypt to the horrors of the Holocaust and the more recent threats, their unwavering determination and courage in the face of adversity shine as a beacon of hope and perseverance for all.

National Resilience — The Key to Winning the War

Miriam Adelson, MD

What Is Resilience?

A CADEMIC LITERATURE DEFINES resilience as the ability of a system to cope successfully with a severe disruption or disaster, maintain reasonable differential functionality during the event, and recover quickly to support growth.

Resilience is not an innate quality. It is necessary to build and maintain resilience over time, according to a detailed and comprehensive plan. This effort benefits the system even if no disaster or disruption ever occurs, although this is something that, unfortunately, almost inevitably does happen.

The key components of resilience are awareness of relevant risks, practical and proactive preparedness and planning according to those risks, strengthening the weak points of the operational plan, leveraging human resources (social capital), inclusive leadership, internal and external connectivity, optimism, and self-assurance.

When discussing national resilience in the Israeli context, it's important to mention the additional components of social solidarity, trust in institutions, the adaptability of the governmental mechanism to the basic needs of the public, and hope for security and socio-economic stability.

Israel, with its long history of facing terror, has no formal recognition of or an organized national effort to build resilience. Instead, Israelis tend to build resilience through the test of adversity and challenging times. These come in many forms; for example the COVID-19 pandemic severely tested Israeli society's resilience, as did the prolonged political crisis that led to five election cycles within three years, and the acute political crisis stemming from the judicial revolution, which began on January 4th of 2023.

A National Trauma

Against the backdrop of these crises, the horrifying events in the Gaza envelope communities on October 7th, and the many casualties resulting from Hamas's attack on civilian settlements, created a national trauma.

Shock, fear, lack of trust in the political leadership, government agencies, and the functioning of the Israel Defense Forces characterized the first stage of the conflict. Israel's national resilience suffered a heavy blow.

Despite this challenging mental state, there have already been several encouraging signs of recovery, which reflect these resilience factors: the remarkable conduct of the Israeli citizens whom Hamas brutally attacked; the effective defense that the communities in the settlements prepared, which saved many civilian lives; and the effective defense of the rapid response teams in the southern communities, which saved so many lives.

And more: The dynamic placement of evacuees from

the Gaza envelope communities into the absorption centers, the widespread voluntary efforts and initiatives of Israeli citizens, the IDF's quick recovery following the initial shock, and the extraordinary support that the US and other Western countries provided — all of these support an effective recovery.

As of this writing, a significant number of Israel's government offices are still struggling to recover from the crisis. Many of them are operating slowly, bureaucratically, and with difficulty. They are not meeting the expectations of Israel's citizens.

Furthermore, this war has already drawn on longer than any previous one — and it's not over yet. The emergency economy is not functioning adequately, and the emergency routine is not yet fully organized, as demonstrated by the fact that thousands of evacuees are still living in temporary housing and hotels, and by the delay in reopening educational institutions.

The State of Israel, like the Jewish people, is known for its high level of social resilience. Jewish history has taught us what adversity is and how to recover quickly. Once we reach the end of this challenging war, we will undoubtedly generate comprehensive recovery.

It is safe to assume that this will lead us to political stability, both domestically and internationally, and to economic growth and renewed prosperity. All of this is within our reach, but it requires careful thought, meticulous planning, and purposeful and well-directed action.

Achieving this outcome is the responsibility of the government. It should be the central role of a civilian cabinet established alongside the national security cabinet. Restoring national resilience is a critical task, no less important than achieving victory on the battlefield.

Israel's Indomitable Spirit: Emerging Stronger from Adversity

Moshe Kaplan, MD

THE OCTOBER 7TH massacre was disastrous for Israel. US Secretary of State Anthony Blinken noted that in proportion to Israel's population of 9.5 million people, it was like experiencing ten 9/11s. The impact has been profound, touching everyone in the country personally.

Such an unprecedented crisis has tested Israel's resilience. The government, military, and citizens were unprepared, and an investigation will undoubtedly follow to understand how this happened and how to prevent future attacks. Yet, despite the immense challenges, one thing remains certain: The strength and spirit of the Israeli people will lead to recovery and growth.

Israel's greatest asset is its people. The unity and determination of its citizens are driving forces that ensure the nation will not only survive but thrive. The Israeli hi-tech ecosystem, including numerous startups, is already mobilizing to support survivors, the injured, soldiers, and civilians still under threat. Even as thousands of rockets target densely populated areas, the focus remains on helping those in need and maintaining the unity of the nation.

The coming weeks will be difficult, but with the rest of society, Israel's hi-tech sector will emerge stronger than before. This sector is pivotal in making Israel is a global leader in developing startups. The country's entrepreneurial ecosystem is built on four fundamental cornerstones, with an additional unique element that sets it apart.

First, the spirit of entrepreneurship in Israel stems from a culture that minimizes the fear of failure. People are more likely to embark on entrepreneurial ventures when their passion outweighs the fear of failure and the cost of alternatives. This cultural trait results in a flourishing startup scene.

Second, Israel benefits from a robust network of investors, especially international ones. Although the current government's judicial reform plans posed challenges to the hi-tech ecosystem, a terror attack will not deter long-term investment. Short-term slowdowns might occur, but the long-term outlook remains positive.

Third, Israel boasts a wealth of talented engineers. The abundance of skilled engineers ensures the continuous advancement of the hi-tech sector.

Fourth, experience plays a crucial role. Serial entrepreneurs, who have multiple ventures under their belts, significantly increase the likelihood of success. The Israeli ecosystem is rich with these experienced entrepreneurs.

These four cornerstones — entrepreneurial spirit, investor support, engineering talent, and experience — are common to other leading tech hubs like San Francisco, Boston, London, and Berlin. However, Israel has a distinctive fifth element: mandatory military service.

This compulsory service cultivates individuals with exceptional resilience, leadership skills, teamwork capabilities, and loyalty. As former Prime Minister Golda Meir famously said, "If the Arabs put down their weapons today, there would be no more violence. If the Jews put down their weapons today, there would be no more Israel." While acting under pressure, as it has had to do recently, the fifth element becomes invaluable as it generates strong, resilient, and better-skilled actors where it matters — people with perseverance, in leadership positions, ready to work in teams, and with extreme loyalty. When the crisis passes, these people use the skills they have honed to contribute to the strength of Israel's hi-tech ecosystem.

The result is a stronger, more innovative, and more resilient nation. Israel will emerge from this crisis fortified and ready for many prosperous years ahead. As the saying goes, tough times create strong people, strong people create easy times, easy times create soft people, and soft people create tough times. Israel is currently in a tough time, but its indomitable spirit ensures that it will not only endure but also thrive.

Building Resilience and Standing Against Hate: WIZO and Hadassah's New Initiatives

Carol Ann Schwartz

WIZO, THE ISRAELI Women's Zionist organization, has unveiled its latest "Emotional Resilience" programs for its educational institutions. It designed these five programs to bolster personal resilience, equip individuals with psychological coping skills, and foster deep connections among participants. This psycho-educational system aims to help individuals navigate trauma effectively, drawing inspiration from WIZO's existing therapy programs.

WIZO, known for its dedication to advancing the status of women and promoting welfare for all sectors of Israeli society, has a long-standing commitment to encouraging Jewish education both in Israel and the Diaspora. The introduction of these new programs signifies a step forward in its support of mental health and resilience within the community in Israel.

In parallel, Hadassah, the Women's Zionist Organization of America, has made significant strides in addressing contemporary issues through the adoption of two new policy statements at its midwinter meetings in West Palm Beach, Florida. These statements, entitled "Condemning Gender-Based Violence" and "Standing Up to Antisemitism on College Campuses and in Communities Around the Country," highlight the organization's proactive stance on pressing social issues.

Hadassah's National President, Carol Ann Schwartz, emphasized the organization's commitment to combating antisemitism, especially in the wake of the October 7, 2023. She stated, "As the largest Jewish women's organization in the country, Hadassah is committed to speaking out against all forms of antisemitism, including the new and alarming surge since Hamas's attack on Israel." Schwartz emphasized that Hadassah will not remain silent in the face of antisemitism, whether it appears on college campuses, at the United Nations, or in any other arena. The organization is intensifying its efforts to educate and empower supporters, build community, and cultivate pride in Zionism.

One of the alarming issues that Hadassah addresses is the horrific acts of sexual violence that Hamas committed against Israeli women and girls. The policy statement "Condemning Gender-Based Violence" calls for justice for the victims and demands a comprehensive investigation into these crimes. Hadassah insists that this investigation should be conducted independently, impartially, and with a trauma-informed approach, free from the biases of the historically anti-Israel Commission of Inquiry on the Israeli-Palestinian Conflict.

The second policy statement, "Standing Up to Antisemitism on College Campuses and in Communities Around the Country," responds to the 388% increase in antisemitic incidents in the United States. Hadassah reaffirms its commitment to countering antisemitism through education and empowerment. The organization urges leaders, particularly those in government and education, to denounce antisemitism in all its forms, including those masked as anti-Zionism. Hadassah calls for increased support and funding for antisemitism education, collaboration with government agencies to address harassment and discrimination, and the adoption of the IHRA definition of antisemitism.

Both WIZO and Hadassah continue to play pivotal roles in advocating for social justice, supporting resilience, and fighting against hate. Their initiatives not only provide immediate support and advocacy but also work toward long-term cultural and educational changes that empower individuals and communities.

Rising from Ruins: The Journey of the Israel Trauma Coalition

Israeltraumacoalition.org

IN 2001, AS the second intifada erupted, the UJA Federation of New York recognized the profound need to offer emotional support to the survivors of the terror attacks engulfing Israel. To address this, it selected seven Israeli organizations that specialized in trauma treatment, and united them under the Israel Trauma Coalition (ITC) banner. It appointed experienced clinical social worker, Talia Levanon, who specialized in grief and crisis, to lead this initiative. Today, she serves as the ITC's CEO.

Talia Levanon's unusual background fashioned her into someone who could have real impact. Born in Switzerland and raised in Nigeria, where her father worked for Teva Pharmaceutical Industries, Levanon moved to Israel as a teenager. After joining the Israel Defense Forces at the onset of the 1973 Yom Kippur War, she served in an intelligence combat unit. Her army experience not only integrated her into Israeli society, but it also foreshadowed her future in trauma care, as she aided those suffering from post-war trauma.

Under Levanon's leadership, the ITC evolved from a modest project with a small grant into a respected international organization. It now serves as an advisory body to the United Nations, assisting first responders in numerous countries during crises such as earthquakes, mass shootings, and terror attacks. The ITC's unique "Israeli" approach to trauma treatment emphasizes strength and resilience over victimhood. This philosophy underscores its mission of cooperation, resilience, and rehabilitation.

One of Levanon's key insights is the necessity of supporting those who assist trauma victims. Recognizing that professionals such as ambulance drivers and social workers endure secondary trauma as a result of their work, the ITC incorporates their care into its programs.

The ITC, in full cooperation with Israel's government ministries, introduced the concept of "resilience centers." The first center opened in 2007 for communities bordering the Gaza Strip, an area that frequently comes under rocket attack following Hamas's takeover of the Palestinian enclave. The ITC located all its centers strategically, in regions with high exposure to security threats. Normally operating during regular hours, they remain open 24/7 in emergencies.

Staffing each resilience center are trauma specialists, including social workers and psychologists, who provide immediate treatment during and after traumatic events. The centers also offer training to keep the staff updated with the necessary skills to treat trauma victims, and work with local authorities to prepare communities for potential emergencies. The need for such preparation became starkly clear during Operation Protective Edge in 2014. The ITC has continued to adapt to the evolving security landscape.

The events of October 7 were a devastating blow for the ITC centers serving the Gaza border communities.

Years of cross-border conflict had already left therapists and residents in the Gaza border region emotionally drained. Hamas's sudden onslaught caught everyone off guard, even as it required the immediate evacuation of all the resilience centers in the affected areas, along with the residents. The attacks shattered basic assumptions of security. Some staff members lost their lives or were kidnapped. Many faced unimaginable trauma.

Amid these challenges, the ITC's work intensified. Levanon reports that while it treated 6,000 people in all of 2022, since October 7, it has assisted 15,000 individuals. On a personal level, Levanon has found solace in her work, which helps her to manage her anxiety and concerns for her relatives and the country.

In the aftermath of the October attacks, the ITC swiftly adapted. In collaboration with the Health Ministry and the National Insurance Institute, it launched a national hotline, *5486, staffed by therapists, to meet the rising demand for trauma support. The ITC dispatched teams to temporary resettlement areas such as Eilat and the Dead Sea to work with evacuated communities.

As residents began to return to their homes, resilience centers in war-torn areas started reopening. Teva Pharmaceuticals partnered with the ITC to recruit and train new therapists, addressing the growing need for trauma treatment.

Levanon acknowledges that neither she nor most of her colleagues have had time for personal mental health support since October 7. The healing process for them, as for the nation, is just beginning. She remains optimistic, emphasizing that resilience means recognizing vulnerability and learning to manage it. The ITC's work is a testament to this resilience, providing hope and support in the face of adversity.

A Beacon of Hope: The Journey of Attorney Hanan Alsanah

Moshe Kaplan, MD

IT WAS EARLY on the morning of October 7th, a day that should have been restful for Attorney Hanan Alsanah, director of the Center for Bedouin Women's Rights at Itach-Ma'aki: Women Lawyers for Social Justice. She had planned a family picnic, a rare break from her demanding work. However, as she prepared for the day, her phone buzzed with an unusual flurry of messages from local WhatsApp leadership groups not typically active on Saturdays. At first, she thought little of the news of the invasion, believing that Israel would swiftly handle whatever disturbance was happening. But as the hours wore on, the gravity of the attack became apparent. Feeling the chaos in the absence of a strong response from the Israeli security services, Alsanah, for first time, contemplated fleeing her home. This gave her a profound sense of insecurity.

Initially, she considered seeking refuge abroad, perhaps taking her children to London until the chaos subsided. But soon, desperate messages poured in from both Jewish and Bedouin survivors, pleading for assistance as the military failed to respond. Women from unrecognized Bedouin villages urgently needed mobile bomb shelters and coverage from the Iron Dome anti-missile defense system. This was a turning point for Alsanah; she abandoned her plans to escape and sprang into action, leveraging her network to coordinate immediate aid.

Alsanah reached out to individuals who could navigate the desert and locate survivors from the Supernova Music Festival near Kibbutz Re'im. Many of these rescuers were Bedouin, well-versed in the terrain. She spent the first day organizing transportation for the injured and those fleeing the area. By the second day, she was arranging deliveries of essential supplies to the most vulnerable Jewish and Bedouin communities. On the third day, alongside her Jewish colleague, Shir Nosatzki, from the organization Have You Seen the Horizon Lately?, she established an emergency situation room in the Bedouin city of Rahat. They united their networks of activists, NGOs, and public representatives to aid both Bedouin families affected by rocket attacks and families from Gaza border communities.

Six months later, this emergency situation room remains a vital resource, particularly for single-mother families in 16 unrecognized Bedouin villages. Here, 37 Bedouin women volunteers, along with their Jewish counterparts, assist approximately 1,000 needy families with basic supplies, emotional support, and legal aid. Although women lead this movement, many men have also joined as volunteers, reflecting a growing communal solidarity.

Alsanah's journey is rooted in her unconventional upbringing. As a child, she assisted her father, a shepherd and community sheikh, with his 100-strong herd in Lod.

She took on responsibilities typically reserved for boys, helping her father at markets and in his mediation tent. This early exposure to leadership and resilience laid the groundwork for her future advocacy.

Breaking barriers, Alsanah earned a law degree from Ben-Gurion University in Beersheva, a remarkable achievement given her traditional Bedouin background. Her determination to be independent and active in her community's welfare drove her forward. Now, she dreams of becoming a judge, and she is proud that her pioneering path has inspired her nieces to pursue higher education; one has even become a lawyer.

In her professional and personal life, Alsanah champions women's rights while honoring her Bedouin heritage. She and her supportive husband, from a feminist Bedouin family, have instilled these values in their four children, encouraging their sons to advocate for gender equality.

Focusing on the unrecognized Bedouin villages, Alsanah's work encompasses promoting civil rights, securing basic services, and engaging with international forums to highlight human rights issues. Over the past 23 years, she has contributed to significant developments such as establishing high schools, clinics, and community centers in these underserved areas. Despite the resistance of some male leaders, she perseveres, earning respect and forging pathways for women's leadership.

Alsanah's resilience and dedication are unwavering. She believes that fostering strong women is key to her own strength. Despite the current conflict with Gaza, which has affected the Bedouin community deeply, she maintains hope, based on the cooperation between Bedouin and Jewish volunteers that she has witnessed. This unity provides a beacon of light amid the darkness, reinforcing her belief that the land belongs to those who care about each other.

Today, Alsanah's mission is to expand this light through collaborative efforts, ensuring that compassion and cooperation prevail over extremism. Her story is a testament to the power of solidarity and the enduring hope for a peaceful, shared society.

Leading the Way Forward: Ben Gurion University's Remarkable Resilience

Sourced from The Hartman Institute event, May 8, 2024

MEET THE BGU students and faculty who are helping the Negev to rebuild and recover:

Alon Jacobs — wounded BGU Industrial Engineering and Management student-reservist
Alon was called up for duty on the morning of October 7th to help secure the kibbutzim Hamas was attacking. He served five military cycles in Gaza before suffering a spinal injury.

Talia Meital Schwartz Tayri, PhD — AI for SW lab at BGU
In the aftermath of the October 7th tragedy, Dr. Tayri created a groundbreaking AI bot designed to support the mental health of survivors, soldiers, and the families of abductees.

Galit Katarivas Levy, PhD — Department of Biomedical Engineering
Dr. Levy created a 3D printed solution to carry medications in the field during war. IDF units across the country now rely on it.

Rising from Ashes: The Inspirational Journey of Israel's Amputee Soccer Team

Moshe Kaplan, MD

When Ben Binyamin was left for dead, his right leg blown off during the Hamas attack on the Tribe of Nova Music Festival, the Israeli professional soccer player thought he would never again play the game he loved. "When I woke up," the 29-year-old said, "I felt I was going to spend the rest of my life in a wheelchair."

However, Binyamin soon learned about a chance to be "normal" again: Israel's national amputee soccer team. The team, which includes three Israeli soldiers who lost limbs fighting in the war with Hamas, has offered these men a chance to heal from the life-altering wounds that they suffered during the Oct. 7 attacks and Israel's ensuing war in Gaza. This team is set to head to France in June for the European Amputee Football Championships, where 16 teams, mostly from Europe, will compete.

"It's the best thing in my life," said 1st Sgt. Omer Glikstal of the team's twice-weekly practices at a stadium in the Tel Aviv suburb of Ramat Gan. The 20-year-old soldier from Haifa regularly played soccer until a rocket-propelled grenade shattered his left foot during a battle in Gaza in November and turned his life upside-down. "It's a very different game than I used to play, but in the end, it's the same," he said.

Dozens of Israelis lost limbs during the Hamas attacks that killed some 1,200 people in southern Israel and the subsequent war. Sheba Medical Center in Ramat Gan, home to a major rehabilitation center, has treated about 60 amputees. Israel's Defense Ministry reports that 1,573 soldiers have been wounded since Israel began its ground offensive in late October, which required troops to engage in close combat with Hamas militants. Of the approximately 320 soldiers who were critically wounded in combat, some are amputees as well.

Israeli athletes and others who lost limbs have benefited from a world-class medical system with decades of experience treating young people injured in Israel's previous wars and conflicts. In Gaza, unknown numbers of Palestinians have also lost limbs in a war that Hamas officials claim has taken 34,000 lives (Israeli's estimates bring the number closer to 20,000, many of whom are militants, not civilians). Gaza's health system has been overwhelmed, and doctors and patients often need to choose between amputation or death. Before the war, Gaza also had a fledgling team of amputee soccer players wounded in previous conflicts with Israel.

Shaked Bitton, an Israeli army division commander, lost his right leg when a Hamas sniper with a .50-caliber round shot him near the Jabaliya refugee camp in late October. "I heard two shots. I fell down. I looked back," the 21-year-old soldier said, "and I saw my leg." Bitton thought his life was over — he had never even met an amputee before — until others who had lost limbs and successfully resumed their lives visited him in the hospital.

Among them was Zach Shichrur, the founder of the soccer team. Severely injured when a bus ran over his foot at age eight, Shichrur knew what Bitton and many others were going through, and he offered them hope. "There is nothing greater than to go out and compete at the international level when you have the Israeli flag on your chest. Most of us, if not all, could not have even imagined something like this," said Shichrur, 36, an attorney and the team's captain. Since its founding five years ago, the Israeli team has met with growing success, placing third in the Nations League in Belgium in October, which qualified it to compete in the European championship in June.

Amputee soccer teams have six field players who are missing lower limbs; they play on crutches and without prosthetics. Each team has a goalkeeper with a missing upper extremity. The pitch is smaller than standard. At team practices, the absence of an arm or a leg, whether from an accident, a war injury, or a birth defect, does not deter the Israeli players. "We all have something in common. We've been through a lot of hard and difficult times. It unites us," said Aviran Ohana, a cybersecurity expert whose right leg is shorter than his left due to a birth defect and who has played with the team for two years.

On a recent April evening, the team started its warm-up with sprints around the pitch, the men speeding forward, propelled by one leg, steadied by their crutches. A game against able-bodied teenagers followed. Binyamin, dripping with sweat, kicked the ball with his left leg as the coach shouted from the sidelines: "Forward! Forward!" The men celebrated every goal.

Sir Ludwig Guttmann, a Jewish neurologist who fled

Nazi Germany in 1939 and settled in Britain, is credited with pioneering competitive sports as a form of rehabilitation. In Israel today, the amputee soccer team offers the players the excitement of competition and the healing powers of sport, said Michal Nechama, the team's physical therapist. "They need it for their souls," she said. "It gives them joy, pride. That extra thing that you can't give in a hospital."

Resilience Amid Adversity: Israel's High-Tech Sector Stands Strong

Moshe Kaplan, MD

Despite the harrowing events of October 7th and the ongoing war in Gaza, Israel's high-tech sector remains a beacon of resilience and innovation. This robust sector, which accounts for nearly half of the country's total exports, continues to attract investors and venture capital, according to a new report from Startup Nation Central (SNC), an Israeli innovation-focused non-profit organization.

One might think that such significant turmoil would dampen investor confidence, but Israel's tech industry has shown remarkable fortitude. While total investment fell by 28% compared to the previous six months — a decline mirroring trends in the US — the value of mergers and acquisitions (M&As) more than doubled, indicating strong long-term confidence in the sector. The prospects for a post-war recovery are encouraging, pointing to sustained growth and innovation.

Investments are the lifeblood of tech companies in Israel, often dubbed the "Startup Nation." In the six months following October 7th, they announced 220 private investment rounds, raising an estimated $3.1 billion. This is a notable decrease from the 330 rounds and $4.3 billion of the previous the six months, yet it underscores the continued flow of capital into the sector. Security technologies, the largest single sector, accounted for over a third of these investments, highlighting the strategic importance of this area in the current global landscape.

Noteworthy investments include a $265 million round for Next Insurance, which develops easy insurance solutions for small businesses, and substantial rounds for cybersecurity company Axonius ($200 million) and VAST Data ($118 million). Despite the challenges, overall investment in Israeli startups has fallen less dramatically than in the US since mid-2022, and the post-October 7th decline has been relatively mild.

Mergers and acquisitions have shown particular resilience. The number of M&As remained stable, with 25 occurring before and 26 after October 7th. Notably, the value of these deals surged from $1.4 billion to $3.7 billion. Significant transactions included the $1 billion acquisition of Resident Home by US-based Ashley Home, and nine deals exceeding $100 million, six of which were in security technologies.

"Despite recent challenges, Israel's tech industry is not just surviving; investment flows and VC activities have remained robust, proving the sector's unflagging innovation excellence," the SNC report states. This resilience is evident when comparing Israeli tech investment trends with those of the US, reaffirming Israel's global standing even in turbulent times.

The tech sector faced additional challenges when the Israel Defense Forces called up 15% of its workforce for reserve duty immediately following October 7th. This created short-term funding gaps, especially for the thousands of smaller startups with limited cash reserves. However, the sector has adapted quickly. Donors have established more than 20 new funds since October 7th, with half specifically addressing urgent funding needs stemming from the war. Collectively, these funds have raised over $1.7 billion, providing a crucial lifeline for struggling startups.

Avi Hasson, CEO of Startup Nation Central, remains optimistic about the future. "Israel continues to attract investors looking for solutions to shared global challenges with high potential opportunities," he says. "With attractive valuations and significant growth potential, the Israeli tech ecosystem is showing characteristic resilience. I anticipate seeing a new wave of innovation — a 'startup baby boom' of tech companies — that will create even more dynamic opportunities for our sector after this war."

In summary, Israel's high-tech sector is demonstrating remarkable resilience amid adversity. The ability to attract significant investments and maintain robust M&A activity underscores the sector's strength and potential for continued innovation and growth, even in the face of profound challenges.

The 48 — 2024

Israel 21c

Every year, in honor of Israel's Independence Day, the publication Israel21c compiles a list of 48 to recognize those who have shown resilience and are helping to build a brighter future for Israel.

1. Danielle Abraham — Rebuilding Israel's ruined farms

On October 7th, Hamas terrorists destroyed farms in the Gaza border area, affecting 70% of Israel's fresh produce. Danielle Abraham, executive director of Volcani International Partnerships, immediately established ReGrow Israel not only to help rehabilitate the ruined farms, but also to bring new innovation to the sector.

2. Talia Levanon — Helping to heal Israel's trauma

As CEO of the Israel Trauma Coalition, Talia Levanon's goal, post October 7th, is to help the people of Israel prioritize strength over victimhood.

3. Yaron Waksman — Surfing as a healer

Yaron Waksman has won several awards as the cofounder

and CEO of HaGal Sheli, an Israeli nonprofit transforming the lives of at-risk youth and special communities, by developing resilience through surfing skills. Following October 7th, he and his organization provided care for over 1,000 evacuees, released hostages, veterans, and Supernova Festival survivors.

4. Lorena Khateeb-Kizel — Druze activist

Lorena Khateeb-Kizel is a Druze Israeli social activist and recipient of awards from the Ministry of Education and the Peres Center for Peace and Innovation, among others. Since October 7, she has been creating trilingual content about Hamas crimes against innocent Israelis that she posts on various Internet platforms with the belief that if she can influence one person, her message will go to dozens more.

5. Israel's reserve soldiers — Saving Israel from disaster

When war broke out in Israel, 360,000 reserve soldiers dropped everything to come and help their country.

6. Cochav Elkayam-Levy, PhD — The voice of Hamas rape victims

Dr. Cochav Elkayam-Levy, an attorney and expert in international law, gender, and human rights defense, heads the Civil Commission on October 7 Crimes by Hamas against Women and Children. This independent collaboration of international human rights experts and women's rights organizations advocates for and supports the investigation of Hamas's war crimes against women and children during the massacre on October 7, 2023, and the on-going war crimes against abducted women and children.

7. Hanadi Sha'er — Campaigning for unity

Hanadi Sha'er, 33, is the first Arab woman to work in policy promotion at the national government level, after leading and managing frameworks for young women at risk from the Arab society in the Negev. Today at AJEEC-NISPED, she helps local communities cope with the aftermath of October 7th.

8. Yaniv Kusevitzky — Using soccer to bring normalcy to children

As CFO of the Equalizer, Yaniv Kusevitzky has been using soccer to help change the lives of underprivileged youngsters from all sectors of Israeli society for many years. Since October 7th, the organization has been bringing normalcy back into their lives and helping often-traumatized children displaced from their homes.

9. Ben Sochman — Keeping the presses running at all costs

Ben Sochman, CEO of Be'eri Print, spent 18 hours with his family trapped in a "safe room" of his Kibbutz Be'eri home on October 7th. Just one week later, he and his team reopened the main business on which the community's livelihood depends, in a true example of Israeli resilience.

10. Shuki Taylor — Urging people to tell their stories

Shuki Taylor, the founder and CEO of M2: The Institute for Experiential Jewish Education, says that in the face of loss and pain, we can cultivate resilience by taking control over our own stories and narratives.

11. Ziv Katzir — Using AI for a better future

Israel's top artificial intelligence policymaker says that innovation is crucial to post-October 7th rebuilding efforts to create better services for all Israeli citizens. His approach involves accelerating existing initiatives, such as the expansion of Israel's computing infrastructure and the facilitation of research scholarships, to expedite progress.

12. Fleur Hassan-Nahoum — Fighting for a pluralistic Jerusalem

Having immigrated to Israel from Gibraltar over 20 years ago, Fleur Hassan-Nahoum is Jerusalem's Deputy Mayor for Foreign Relations, Economic Development, and Tourism, as well as cofounder of the UAE-Israel Business Council and the Gulf Israel Women's Forum. Her front is the international media, where she has a platform to tell the truth about Israel. She is constantly working on how to represent the country's trauma, loss, and tragedy, and the geopolitical reality in the best way possible.

13. Rachel Goldberg-Polin — Fighting tirelessly to bring her son home

Rachel Goldberg-Polin has spent every day since Hamas kidnapped her son Hersh on October 7th in an unflagging campaign to free her son and the other hostages. In April, *Time Magazine* selected her as one of the 100 most influential people of 2024.

14. Tomer Dror & Shir Diner — Strengthening the home front

Tomer Dror is the CEO of Lev Echad (One Heart), an organization that focuses on building the resilience of Israeli society, the Jewish people, and the Western world, through the deployment of volunteers in emergency situations. As the COO of One Heart, Shir Diner has visited Ukraine 12 times, and she led emergency delegations to Turkey and Morocco, before taking on her greatest challenge following October 7, in her home country.

15. Dorit Admony Chasnoff — Organizing equipment and food

Dorit Admony Chasnoff, an artist, spiritual mentor, cooking teacher, and mother of four, says that passion drove her to organize food, equipment, and supplies for soldiers and displaced families after October 7th.

16. Hanan Alsanah — Bedouin lawyer helping Oct. 7th victims

Attorney Hanan Alsanah, director of the Center for

Bedouin Women's Rights, admits that she nearly lost hope after the Hamas attack. Instead, she threw herself into the aid effort, helping Bedouin and Jewish victims alike.

17. Brothers and Sisters in Arms — Leading the volunteers

Brothers and Sisters in Arms started out as a protest group, but on October 7th pivoted to giving Israelis aid exactly where they needed it most — from evacuations, to clothing and furniture drives, to feeding the needy and helping the farmers. Their incredible volunteer response helped the country survive its toughest days.

18. Sylvan Adams — Rebuilding Israel better than ever

Philanthropist and Israel advocate Sylvan Adams has initiated many large-scale projects that show off the beauty of Israel to international audiences. Since the outbreak of war, he is investing heavily in rebuilding the south. He aims to tackle international prejudices and build a stronger Israel.

19. Dror Bin — The man steering Israel's high-tech ship

As CEO of the Israel Innovation Authority, Dror Bin has never known normal times, but he's convinced that Israel can ride out any storm. He cites Winston Churchill, who famously said, "Every crisis is an opportunity." Israel has had more than its fair share of crises, but emerges stronger from each one. Less than a month after October 7th, the IIA swung into action with a $100 million fund to help early-stage startups, as many had less than six months of "runway" — money for salaries and other essentials — after potential investors froze, waiting to see what would happen.

20. Oded Ronen — Choreography for the missing

Choreographer and political activist Oded Ronen is a leader of the missing persons unit in the aftermath of October 7. He directed an animation video, *They Are US*, that went viral globally in 18 languages. He choreographed *The Missings* for Ulm Theater Ballet in Germany about human resilience in the missing persons unit.

21. Dr. Khalil Bakly — Advocating for a shared life

A longtime social and political activist, Dr. Khalil Bakly, one of the leaders of the HaBustan community in Nof HaGalil, is advocating for a shared Arab-Jewish life more intently than ever in the aftermath of the October 7th attack.

22. Tali Groshaus — Helping the evacuees

As head of mission for Israel Emergency Response at IsraAID, Tali Groshaus usually focuses on projects in Latin America and the Caribbean. All that changed on October 7th, when she found herself back at home with her team, responding to the unprecedented violent attack and the crisis-affected communities, helping to meet their urgent needs and rebuild their future.

23. Matan Peretz — Reservist, comedian

Returning from his Mexican vacation directly into war and army reserve service, comedian Matan Peretz uses social media to make us laugh at harsh moments while fighting for the truth.

24. Dorit Gvili — Fighting to bring the Gaza hostages home

Since October 7th, ad exec Dorit Gvili has made it her mission to make sure hostage families' voices are heard and the hostages in Gaza not forgotten. She works with the families to create ad campaigns, etc. that educate the global public and build up activism to support the return of the hostages to their families.

25. Joseph Gitler — Feeding Israel and helping the farms

Joseph Gitler founded and runs Leket Israel, the largest food-rescue organization in Israel. Following October 7th, Leket and its nonprofit partners evaluated the most pressing needs and reconfigured operations to offer emergency relief on multiple fronts.

26. Mishy Harman — Telling the Israel story

Mishy Harman is the cofounder, host, and CEO of Israel Story, the most listened-to Jewish and Israeli podcast in the world, with hundreds of thousands of listeners in more than 190 countries. After October 7th, Israel Story pivoted its entire operation and started producing daily

"Wartime Diaries," which are an attempt to capture slivers of life during these difficult days. The sense of volunteerism and community we experienced in the wake of October 7th is a hopeful reminder of what our society can be at its best. Indeed, that notion of "being in it together" has, to a certain extent, managed to bridge deep societal divides.

27. Zeev Engelmayer — Optimistic art-ivist

Zeev "Shoshke" Engelmayer's brightly colored postcards dedicated to the hostages in Gaza have captured our hearts in moments of shared pain and above all — hope.

28. Erel Margalit — Healing the high-tech sector

Erel Margalit's efforts since the October 7th attacks have reinforced his role as a prominent figure within Israel's high-tech ecosystem. He has been rallying support for employees and families affected by October 7th and the ensuing war, ensuring their well-being and providing financial stability during a challenging period. He has brought together CEOs, business leaders, and stakeholders to develop strategies for navigating the uncertainties and disruptions.

29. Yocheved Kim Ruttenberg — Volunteer leader

Three days after October 7, Yocheved Kim Ruttenberg flew to Israel with $17,000 that she had raised on social media, and 23 duffel bags full of supplies. Today she is managing volunteer efforts in Israel.

30. Ella Rose Azaria — Swim coach, environmentalist

Climate change and social activist Ella Rose Azaria has been sharing her experience as a certified master swimming coach to help Israeli internal refugees cope with trauma and anxiety.

31. David Bedein — A warning voice about UNRWA

David Bedein, MSW, is a community organizer and founding director of the Israel Resource News Agency, as well as head of the Nahum Bedein Center for Near East Policy Research. He has been fighting to reveal the truth about UNRWA for years, an effort that has taken on even more urgency since the revelations following October 7.

32. HaShoteret Az-Oolay — Handing out love at Israel's civil protests

Az-Ooly, a clown "police officer," is a regular fixture at Jerusalem demonstrations, offering unexpected love and humor to police and protestors, in an effort to defuse tensions and bring people together, both before and after the attacks.

33. Nitzan Mintz & Dede Bandaid — Making people look twice

Married couple Nitzan Mintz, a visual poet, and Dede Bandaid, the pseudonym of one of Tel Aviv's best-known street artists are partners in the Tel Aviv-created

#KidnappedFromIsrael guerrilla poster campaign that has spread worldwide.

34. Hagai Levine, MD — Health champion

Chairman of the Israeli Association of Public Health Physicians, Dr. Hagai Levine leads the health team of the Hostages and Missing Families Forum and initiated the transfer of medications to the hostages in Gaza.

35. Solomon Geveye — Blazing a high-tech trail for Ethiopian Israelis

Ethiopian entrepreneur Solomon Geveye has set up a new venture fund to encourage more Ethiopians into Israel's high-tech community, and, war or no war, he's determined to achieve this goal.

36. Mohammad Darawshe — Helping to keep the peace

Aside from offering shelter to evacuees from southern Israel in the wake of the Hamas attack, peace activist Mohammad Darawashe played a significant role in dousing the flames of internal conflict between Israel's Jewish and Arab populations.

37. Yael Yechieli — Supporting reservist families

This social activist, feminist, and gender equity specialist is deeply passionate about advocating for equality and social justice. In response to October 7th, she co-founded an organization dedicated to supporting reserve soldiers' families who found themselves functioning as single-parent homes.

38. Chen Linchevski, Gil Friedlander, Jason Wolf — Creating an Iron Nation

In response to the need that arose after October 7th, these three seasoned Israeli entrepreneurs founded Iron Nation. They have recruited experienced and creative high-tech professionals and investors to support promising Israeli startups put at risk when their workers joined the reserves to defend their country.

39. Talia Meital Schwartz-Tayri, PhD — Melding tech and psychology

Following October 7, Dr. Talia Schwartz-Tayri developed AI-based technological systems for the evacuee local authorities and for psychological first-response via WhatsApp. She was recently honored at Ben-Gurion University for International Women's Day.

40. Tania Coen-Uzzielli — Finding solace in art

Tania Coen-Uzzielli immigrated to Israel from Italy in 1983 and has been Tel Aviv Museum of Art's director since January 2019. She believes in the transformative power of art as a source of healing, solace, and strength in times of adversity. She has helped to develop various initiatives that create a safe haven for the processing of trauma, utilizing observation, discussion, and the therapeutic power of art as essential tools.

41. Prof. Daniel Chamovitz — Fostering unity in the south

Prof. Chamovitz, the President of Ben-Gurion University in Beersheva, says the university is deeply committed to rebuilding and revitalizing not only the local Negev community but also contributing to the broader fabric of Israeli society.

42. Sarale Shadmi Wortman — Community builder

As a founder of the Varda Institute, an organization dedicated to building community, Sarale Shadmi Wortman and her colleagues instituted a unique model to help communities reconnect, rebuild routines, and grow stronger in a culture of belonging that creates community support during wartime.

43. Tasha Cohen — A traveling holistic clinic for soldiers

Tasha Cohen, 38, a former Londoner, founded Chayal's Angels following October 7. She organized volunteer therapists into a traveling holistic clinic to treat and heal Israeli soldiers fighting along the northern border.

44. Erez Kaganovitz — Humans of October 7th

A native Tel Avivian photojournalist and TEDx speaker, Erez Kaganovitz is the human behind the Humans of Tel Aviv, Humans of Israel, and Humans of the Holocaust, as well as the Humans of October 7th project, which brings to light the stories of the unique Israelis who stood up against terrorism. It showcases Israeli DNA at its best and highlights the incredible spirit and resilience of the Israeli people.

45. Mor Assia & Shelly Hod Moyal — Investment angels

The partners behind iAngels say that the strength of their portfolio companies and of their own team, which continued to do business while dealing with reserve duty and other hardships during the war in Gaza, inspired the creation of this new investment fund.

46. Michal Levit — Cooking up culinary comfort

Michal Levit is director of programs and innovation at Asif: Culinary Institute of Israel, which opened its kitchens in the wake of October 7 to provide support and comfort through food.

47. Nitsana Darshan-Leitner — Using the law to fight terror

As president of Tel Aviv-based Shurat HaDin—Israel Law Center, attorney Nitsana Darshan-Leitner has represented hundreds of terror victims in legal actions against terror organizations and their supporters. Shurat HaDin utilizes court systems around the world to go on the legal offensive against Israel's enemies, defending against lawfare suits, fighting academic and economic boycotts, and challenging those who seek to delegitimize the Jewish state.

48. Hadassa Goldberg — Helping through community

Through her on-line posts, social-media influencer Hadassa Goldberg gives her online community opportunities to help in Israel and the ability to understand what Israelis are going through.

A Story of Unity and Hope: Surviving Hamas Captivity

Amelie Botbol

Jewish News Syndicate, May 14, 2024 (excerpts)

"OUR UNITY GIVES us as much protection as our army. We need it just as much to secure our existence," Sapir Cohen shared with JNS on Monday. Cohen, who endured 55 days of captivity under Hamas, knows firsthand the importance of unity. Her story begins on the eve of Simchat Torah, October 6, when she and her boyfriend, Alex Trufanov, traveled to Kibbutz Nir Oz to celebrate the holiday with his parents.

Loud explosions shattered their morning peace. "We hid under the bed. There was nowhere else to hide. Then, I heard screams of 'Allahu Akbar.' Terrorists were yelling and there were cries of victims they were executing. I quickly understood that they were entering every house and showering the room with bullets. We waited for our turn," Cohen recalled. Soon, the terrorists shot through the door, breaking everything inside before capturing Cohen and Trufanov.

"Alex started screaming as they began to hit him. I was rolled in a blanket. They removed it and took me," she said, her voice trembling with the memory. Cohen saw

Trufanov on his knees, his face covered in blood, being taken away by two armed terrorists. He remains in the Gaza Strip to this day.

Her captors put Cohen on a motorcycle and drove her into Gaza, where she would spend nearly eight harrowing weeks. "At the beginning of my captivity, I kept asking G-d why He had to bring me to that place. Soon enough, it became clear. I was being held with hostages who were doing much worse emotionally, and I made it my mission to bring them hope," Cohen told JNS.

Upon her release, Cohen continued her mission of spreading hope, believing that the unity of the people of Israel is crucial for protection against their enemies. She has been traveling extensively to share her story with Jewish communities around the world. "They need to hear it from us; they can't relate from watching television. Since I started going, we have been getting contributions and a lot of delegations of volunteers are coming to Israel to help," she explained.

In Israel, Cohen actively participates in weekly unity rallies that advocate for the release of hostages. These rallies are a part of her coping and rebuilding process. "We can't sit home in silence and fear. We need to go out and interact with secular and religious people, hear prayers, and hear the words of bereaved and hostage families. We can't have unity from one day to the next, but we can start to build back," she emphasized.

As Israel marked its first post-October 7 Independence Day, Cohen highlighted the importance of celebrating the Jewish people's right to self-determination in the State of Israel. She was among thousands attending an event in Latrun, west of Jerusalem, organized by 44 NGOs. "We are embarking on a series of joint actions and calls, aiming to create a momentum that will restore the spirit and hope for millions of Israeli citizens," stated David Solomon, CEO of Nifgashim, and Yoel Zilberman, CEO and founder of HaShomer HaChadash.

Soldiers wounded in the ongoing war against Hamas also addressed the crowd, emphasizing the heavy emotional cost of the war and the enduring hope. "We have paid and continue to pay the highest price of all. We call upon our wonderful people, together with the immense pain and longing, to be filled with hope," said Brig. Gen. (res.) Dedi Simchi, a former Fire and Rescue Services commissioner whose paratrooper son, Guy, was killed fighting terrorists at the Nova Music Festival on October 7.

"This Independence Day carries significance and unity with a question of how we can be better and become an even more independent country full of meaning," Simchi added. The event featured symbolic acts of solidarity, such as flying kites for the hostages still held in Gaza, and prayers for their safe return and the success of the IDF soldiers.

"This event is meant to remind everyone to have hope and that we must rebuild and be better," Cohen said, adding a powerful message for the leaders of Israel: "Before making any decision, make unity your first priority and make sure that this is the message you are sending the people of Israel."

The Heroic Escape of Yarin Shriki: A Tale of Survival and Strength

Amelie Botbol
Jewish News Syndicate, May 29, 2024 (excerpts)

THE NOVA FESTIVAL massacre on October 7 in Re'im left an indelible mark on those who were present. Hamas terrorists launched an indiscriminate attack, causing the deaths, injuries, and kidnappings of hundreds of party-goers. Amidst the horror of Simchat Torah, tales of survival emerged, showcasing the resilience and courage of individuals who escaped the devastation. One such story is that of Yarin Shriki, a 23-year-old world-champion Israeli jiu-jitsu practitioner.

Yarin Shriki had recently accomplished the significant feat of winning the gold medal in the under-69 kg Gi category at the Paris Grand Prix, marking his third victory in this prestigious event. Shriki's accolades include numerous medals and titles, making him one of Israel's rising martial arts stars. He was the first sabra to win a gold medal at the European Championships and has been crowned Israeli champion four times by the Ayelet Sports Association.

Reflecting on the tragic day, Shriki attributed his survival to his dedication to jiu-jitsu. "The only thing that was lucky for me that day was my love of sports," he said. Shriki, who has always taken great care of himself and dedicated his life to jiu-jitsu, was not one to frequent parties and festivals. However, following a complicated surgery that left him bedridden for a period, his brothers, Idan and Sharon, encouraged him to get out and enjoy life a bit more. They convinced him to join them at the Nova Music Festival, with the agreement that he would drive his own car to the Gaza border area so that he could leave whenever he felt necessary.

On the night of the festival, Shriki and his brothers stayed close to a group of five friends. Around 6:30 a.m., chaos erupted as rockets and drones began raining down on the party. Unlike many of the attendees, Shriki was sober and immediately grasped the gravity of the situation. His jiu-jitsu training kicked in, allowing him to stay calm and focus on the immediate need to survive. He took charge, ensuring that his group didn't panic or scatter, which probably saved their lives.

As he assessed the situation, Shriki's discipline and quick thinking helped the group to avoid the terrorists who were lying in wait. Despite the urge to escape immediately, Shriki decided they should delay before fleeing, a decision that proved crucial. Eventually, gunfire forced the group to split up. Seizing the moment, Shriki drove through a potato field to Kibbutz Tze'elim, about 40 km from the festival site, ensuring his and a friend's safety.

While Shriki and his friend found refuge at the kibbutz, his brothers managed to reach their family home in Netanya. The family's reunion was filled with tears as they recounted their harrowing escape. Shriki now grapples with survivor's guilt, questioning why he survived while others did not. He believes that his unwavering commitment to sports kept him alive, enabling him to remain clear-headed and responsive under pressure.

Six weeks after the massacre, Shriki returned to training, driven by a desire to honor his friends who had been killed or taken hostage. Despite the psychological scars, he remains focused on his goal. Before each match, he seeks strength from the memory of his best friend, Yochai, who was murdered at Nova.

Shriki's determination culminated in another gold medal victory. Standing on the podium, he dedicated his triumph to his lost friends, Yochai ben Zakaria and Osher Simcha Barzilai, as the Israeli flag was hoisted and "Hatikva" played. His story is a testament to the unifying power of sports and the resilience of the human spirit in the face of unimaginable adversity.

Stunning Speech by Menahem Kalmanson, October 7th Hero, Upon Receiving the Israel Prize for Civic Heroism

Yehuda Dov
VINnews, May 15, 2024

Menahem Kalmanson, a member of "Team Elhanan," a family unit that bravely entered Kibbutz Be'eri on Oct. 7th, fought terrorists, and rescued over 100 members of the kibbutz, spoke at the Israel prize ceremony after the team received the Civic Heroism prize for its efforts. Terrorists killed Menahem's eldest brother, Elhanan, hy"d, after 16 hours of fighting. Elhanan is survived by his wife and six children.

Rabbi Kalmanson said, "This ceremony answers the question 'Why are we here?', a question that echoed throughout the past year as dissension and dispute raged in the country and threatened to tear us apart from within. The question, 'Are we still brothers?' continued to echo until the sirens of Simchat Torah echoed and our enemies awaiting our demise came out of their trenches and attacked.

"On Shabbat afternoon my older brother Elhanan, who is so sorely missed by me at this moment, called on me and Itiel [a nephew] to go with him to the south. Despite the fear he chose to go in time after time. We didn't ask ourselves why we are doing this — settlers going out to save secular kibbutzniks. In the middle of the night, we were already very tired but we couldn't stop, as my brother Itiel said, 'When you know your brother is in danger you don't really have a choice. I seek my brothers.'

"When we reached the home of the Meir family in Beeri, Michal refused to open the door. She begged from behind the door, 'Speak so that I can hear your Hebrew,' and she didn't open until I cried, '*Shma Yisrael Hashem Elokeinu Hashem Echad*' and then the door opened immediately. I admit, it wasn't a prayer, it was a cry: I'm a Jew, I'm here for you, please open the door. This call, this cry for unity, echoed around the region that day as thousands of soldiers went out of a sense of deep responsibility and endangered their lives for their brothers. This point which we nearly lost — the sense of brotherliness and mutual fate.

"Elhanan knew the difficulties and weaknesses of this nation and still chose to enter the kibbutz, as he knew the people of Israel deserve this. In the last few months as dissension arose again, we — the bereaved families, met the families of the hostages from such different backgrounds and with so much pain. Everyone there was concerned about the country, lives, hostages, and we had such different views. We listened, argued, looked one another in the eyes, and became full of love which led us to humility. As with all brotherly love, you can't always explain what makes your brother so unique and why he has no possible exchange, as he is a brother."

Kalmanson concluded by saying, "We cannot continue to fight without seeing the good in this nation, as the blood of our brothers cries out from the ground, as we are our brother's keeper."

We Are a Miracle

Yaakov Shwekey
Composed by Yitzy Waldner
Lyrics by Sophia Franco

A nation in the desert
We started out as slaves
Made it to the motherland,
and then came the Crusades
It's been so many years
crying so many tears
don't you know
don't you really know?
We are pushed to the ground
through our faith we are found
standing strong.

The Spanish inquisition
wanted us to bow
But our backs ain't gonna bend
Never then, and never now
It's been so many years
crying so many tears
don't you know
don't you really know?

We are pushed to the ground
through our faith we are found
standing strong.

CHORUS 1:
We are a miracle
We are a miracle
We were chosen with love
And embraced from above
We are a miracle.

Extermination was the plan
When the devil was a man
Ohhh ohhh
But the few who carried on
Live for millions who are gone
It's been so many years
crying so many tears
Don't you know,
don't you really know?
Generations have passed
Only we're here to last....
Standing strong.

We are a miracle
We are a miracle
We were chosen with love
And embraced from above
We are a miracle.

Every day we fight a battle
On the news we are the stars
As history repeats itself

And makes us who we are
Hate is all around us
But we'll be here to sing this song…

We are a miracle
We are a miracle
Through it all, we remain…
Who can explain?
We are a miracle…

What It Means to Choose Life

Douglas Murray

Douglas Murray, a Free Press columnist, received the Alexander Hamilton Award for his "unwavering defense of Western values." This is adapted from his acceptance speech.

I'VE NEVER SEEN as much of the best and the worst of humankind as I have in the past six months in Israel and Gaza. I was here in New York on October 7. On October 8, I went down to Times Square, where there were men and women waving signs celebrating the massacre of the previous day. They weren't calling for a two-state solution. They weren't saying that we'd awfully like to do some borderline territory swaps in the West Bank. No, no. It was all celebrating the massacre.

Some of them were holding these signs in Times Square saying, "By any means necessary," at a time when we already knew what those means included — and, in fact, when the massacre was still going on. I thought then — and I said this in the *Post* — that a few things were obvious. The first was that I had to get to Israel as soon as I could. The second was that we were going to see a kind of Holocaust denialism in real time, and therefore I thought I should see with my own eyes everything that had happened, everything I could see. And the third was that I noticed already what I had said shortly after October 7: that there are some times in your life when a flare goes up and everybody can be seen precisely where they're standing. That seemed to be exactly what had happened.

I went straight to the sites of the massacres, to the hospitals where the wounded were recovering. I won't give you all of the — or even any of the — terrible stories you can hear. From there, I joined the experts — I joined the pathologists in the morgues of Tel Aviv as they were trying to identify the dead, an unbelievable task, which they do with extraordinary delicacy and religiosity, actually. I spent a lot of time with the families of the kidnapped and with the survivors of the Nova party. But I also had the great opportunity to witness firsthand Israel's response — because unlike some countries today, Israel doesn't just sit back with equanimity when it's attacked, much as some of the world would like it to do.

I saw one of the fences that the terrorists broke into on October 7 — and I thought immediately, as well, [that] after the seventh, people aren't going to realize the scale of this: this was a 4,000-person battalion-size terrorist attack that aimed to go all the way up the center of the country. I felt rather proud, actually, to go back through that fence with the IDF when they were going into Gaza in search of the hostages.

I saw the tunnel networks that Hamas has spent all these years building with your money and mine. I have a friend from the British Army, Colonel Richard Kemp. One day, we were standing beneath one of the tunnels that Yahya Sinwar had built — he's the mastermind of the attacks on the seventh — and which he had been videoed going through. I said to Richard, who, like me, is a fan of dark humor, "This is about the size and width of the London Underground." And he said, "Yeah, and I hear it's even longer than the London Underground." I had the opportunity to say, "And I think it's rather better run."

I suppose I can say, as much as anyone, that I saw it all. On the day I left Israel, a few days ago, I was the first person allowed in to see the Hamas terrorists who'd committed the atrocities of October 7 in the prison cells in which they're held. I mention all this, really, to say, what do I make of all this? I'm going to quote Scripture.

I think often of the line from Deuteronomy when G-d says, "I have set before you life and death, blessing and cursing; therefore choose life, that you and your descendants might live." And I think also of the psalmist who said, "I shall not die, but I shall live." Because when I think of October 7 now, I don't think only of the victims; I think of the extraordinary heroes. And I want to mention them to you above all. A young man, a friend of mine in his thirties, woke up in Jerusalem on October 7, realized the seriousness of what was going on, got into his car, drove south, collected some guns, left a farewell message to his children and his wife on his phone.

On the road, he got a call from his company commander, saying, "You have to come back to base in Jerusalem. And he said, "No, we are needed in the south now." And his battalion commander said, "Are you defying an order?" He said, "Yes, I'm defying an order. We are needed in the south." And he fought for the next forty-eight hours and survived.

I think of my friend Moshe, whom I've had the great good fortune of being with for many months. He's now my cameraman and was from the beginning. The first day we were together, we donned our battle armor and helmets on the Gaza border. And I noted that Moshe had a bullet mark down the top of his helmet, and he hadn't mentioned anything about it. I asked, "Where's that from?" He explained that it was from October 7. Every Saturday, he would go down to see a friend of his — who was also in the media — in Kfar Aza, and he drove right into the middle of the firefight on the highway.

He got out and fought and killed three terrorists with his own gun that he carries with him, thank goodness. He fought for the next two days. And he doesn't expect any applause for it or anything like that; he just did what he had to do. I think of the extraordinary Druze men who provided the food at the Nova party and whom I met a few months ago, some weeks after the atrocities, and who described to me not just what they'd seen at the party — which the world was already trying to deny — but what they'd done. They didn't see themselves as heroes at all, but because they could understand Arabic, they saved many young Jews that morning. I asked them, "Why, among other things, did you do it?" They're proud Israelis, they're Druze. They said, "The Hamas hate us even more than they hate the Jews."

I think of the Muslim doctor whom Hamas held as a human shield at one point in the morning. Even after being wounded, he saved the lives of other Israelis. I think of the extraordinary people of the United Hatzalah, a sort of first-responders unit: they all get an alert on their phones. They all go off and address a car crash. I spoke to the head of that organization in Jerusalem. He said, "In thirty years of doing this job, the whole thirty years altogether wasn't like one minute that morning.

The lights just went off everywhere." And I think of a young woman called Adi Baruch. She was 23, and I was with her family in December in Judea and Samaria. She was a beautiful girl, a photographer — she decided that she had to go and reenlist after October 7. And she did. Her parents begged her not to, but she said that she had to. She was killed on her first day by a rocket that landed on her in Sderot. Her parents shared with me the note that she'd left for them, in case she didn't make it. In it, she said, among other things, how sorry she was, but she said, "I wanted to live life, and now I want you to live it for me."

I think, finally, of an extraordinary evening in November last year. I was at the Schneider Children's [Medical Center] when the helicopters came, returning the first hostages, the first children whom Hamas had stolen from their homes in the south. We'd been waiting for them for two days. There were two days of thwarted exchanges, where Hamas deliberately eked it out and eked it out — more and more torture for families. But when the helicopters emerged — there were two of them, and they emerged in the night sky. The people of Tel Aviv realized what was happening, and every car stopped. I was standing right on top of the hospital, and every single car in Tel Aviv stopped. Suddenly, I noticed applause from the citizens, the Tel Avivians. Then there was singing, singing all the way through the streets of Tel Aviv. I asked my cameraman, "What are they singing?"

They were singing a song, *Hevenu Shalom Aleichem* — "We brought you peace." I learned afterward from speaking to the helicopter commander that there was intense competition among the helicopter pilots to have the good fortune and honor of returning these children home. Now, there are millions of stories like this across Israel. The country rings with them, it resounds with them. It makes me think a lot about home, my home here in America, my home in the UK. There have been polls over the last couple of years asking Americans and British people, "What would you do if your country was invaded?" Two years ago, when Ukraine was invaded, there was a poll here in the U.S. that found — I don't want to make a partisan point but let me risk it —it turned out that a minority of Democrat voters said that they would stay and fight for their country. A slight majority of Republican voters said that they would, but it ended up with only 52 percent of the American public saying that they would stay and fight.

I assume that the rest would hotfoot it to Canada, assuming that Canada wasn't the one invading, which is one of the very few things in geopolitics I like to hold. But when I looked at those polls in the UK, there was an even worse one a few months ago. The pollsters told young British people that the defense secretary said that there was a possibility that we might have to have enlistment in the UK for young people; a mere 27 percent of young people said that they would be willing to be enlisted to fight for their country. These, I don't need to tell you, are not good results. And they bring a whole set of questions, some of which I wrote about in my most recent book. It doesn't surprise me that a lot of young Americans wouldn't be willing to fight for their country if they've been told from the cradle that their country was rotten from birth and had nothing going for it other than slavery, colonialism, and everything else. You've really got to miseducate Americans into this kind of self-loathing.

But I compare this to what I've seen in the last six months. Actually, a number of my readers and viewers have said to me in the last six months, "You've changed, Douglas." I sometimes ask them what it is they mean, and they say, "You've lost some of your pessimism."

I've said to them, there's a reason for that. And the reason is what I've seen in the Israeli public, because actually this wasn't theoretical. It wasn't a poll question. It wasn't some dolts on an American campus, cosplaying being terrorists for the day. Their pathetic attempts — I mean, what's the latest one? They're now in L.A., doing calls to prayer. There's a guy in New York who's got a belly button and a crop top. And at the beginning of this academic year, he was on camera calling for climate emergency, and now he's for Hamas. And I suppose he's "Queers for Palestine" and "Chickens for KFC" and all that.

I would love to drop him into Gaza, although, as I've occasionally said, I'm not sure that there are very many tall buildings to throw him off. But once they rebuild them, that guy will have about a day. He'll be introduced to the elevator fast, I reckon. One of the great things about Israel at the moment is what my friend Bari Weiss said when she arrived in February: "Isn't it wonderful to be a country where nobody gives a damn about woke?" It's so true. Nobody bothers about pronouns. Life is too serious. Reality: it's right in front of you. It seems to me there's a lesson in this, and it's not a lesson for Israel. It's a lesson for us, for you and me, if we are going to restore countries like Great Britain and the United States of America. I spoke some months ago with an older guy in Tel Aviv who said that he'd fought in the 1967 and the 1973 wars. He said, "I owe the younger generation in Israel an apology. I used to say that they didn't have it in them... they like partying. They like being on Instagram and TikTok." And he said, "I owe them an apology. They've been magnificent." And the thing is, perhaps it does require life to become serious again. Perhaps the students we see at these destroyed universities just need a dose of reality someday. I always pray that that day never comes to them, because it'll be the biggest wake-up call anyone has ever had. But all I would say is that this country and Great Britain should be so lucky as to have a young generation like the one in Israel. They were weighed in the balance since October 7, and they've been found to be magnificent.

    What I wanted to say, really, in closing, is that question, I suppose, of Oriana Fallaci's. I wonder what I've learned about life. And I'm going to give you, I'm afraid, a circular definition: that life has to be fought for and has to be cherished. And that's what Israel has been up against: a cult of death, a cult that wishes to annihilate an entire race, and which, after dealing with that race, has made very clear what it wants to do with Christians, everyone in Britain, everyone in America, and everyone else next. They don't hide it at all. We are merely stupid in not believing them. I suppose for those people in America who don't believe them, I say slumber on as long as you can.

Chapter Six

Unity —
The Saving Grace

"When you love someone, you love them as they are, not as you would like them to be."
— Leo Tolstoy

Unity

Moshe Kaplan, MD

It has been said that if we were completely alike, we couldn't communicate, but if we were exactly the same, there would be no need, as we would have nothing to say. Our differences are what allow us to unite.

A nation, like a family, doesn't always have to be perfect or always in agreement, but it must always be united.

Doron Almog, incoming Jewish Agency chairman, revealed his two commitments — or "lives," as he calls them — that define his professional and personal life. One is the army; the other is being an active advocate for the disabled in Israel through his establishment of the ADI Negev-Nahalat Eran organization in honor of his son.

"My life is dedicated to the disabled like my son Eran, and maybe now I am taking [on] a 'third commitment': to strengthen the Jewish people by becoming chairman of the Jewish Agency," he said.

We need to unite to guarantee our existence. Almog says, "We need to guarantee that this state, this only Jewish state, will not only survive and prevail against a threat from Iran, Hezbollah, Hamas, missiles, [foreign] military, attacks, and war, but also a split society."

Almog emphasizes that "we need to unite our people, and we do not have the privilege to lose one segment [of it]. We need to unite all of us: The Orthodox, Conservative, Reform, traditional, secular — together. To be united, one people — a strong people — in order to guarantee our existence by this unity."

A Message of Hope: Reclaiming Our Stories

Moshe Kaplan, MD

T̲h̲e̲ ̲r̲e̲a̲c̲t̲i̲o̲n̲s̲ ̲o̲f̲ Angelica Gottlieb's colleagues at her London start-up where she worked made Hamas's horrific attack even more distressing. They began posting blatantly pro-Hamas content on social media, casting Jews and Israelis as monolithic "white colonizers."

Seeing this narrative play out online, Gottlieb felt compelled to act. She and her friend, Ariella Goodman, decided to use their experiences to educate the public about Zionism and Jewish history. In early March, they launched an Instagram page called Our Shared Jewish History. Their mission: to share stories of those affected by the October 7 attack, highlighting the rich and diverse tapestry of Jewish and Israeli life.

By sharing these personal stories, Gottlieb and Goodman aim to counter simplistic and harmful stereotypes about Jews and Israelis. They believe in giving a voice to the voiceless and showcasing the unique and varied backgrounds that make up Jewish and Israeli history.

Gottlieb and Goodman's friendship began in 2020, when they both joined the Youth Peace Initiative, a Dutch-based Israeli-Palestinian peacebuilding program.

They discovered a surprising connection: their grandmothers had met and become friends at the Jewish World Congress in Prague in 1948. This personal link deepened their bond and commitment to sharing their heritage.

Throughout their time with the Youth Peace Initiative, Gottlieb and Goodman became acutely aware of the way that their identities as English-speaking Israeli immigrants made others question their Jewish-Israeli heritage. Gottlieb, then a Tel Aviv University graduate with a background in social justice and tech, and Goodman, an IDF veteran and history scholar, often discussed the complex issues of Israeli and Palestinian indigeneity.

The rhetoric they faced, especially in left-wing spaces, painted all Jews in Israel as European colonizers who had stolen land from Palestinians. This narrative ignored the area's geopolitical history as well as the diversity within Jewish and Israeli society, which includes people from multiple religions and backgrounds. Gottlieb and Goodman found this not only inaccurate but also deeply hurtful.

Motivated to challenge these misconceptions, they left their respective jobs and focused on their new project. Their Instagram page began with the story of Alex Dancyg, a 75-year-old Polish-Israeli grandfather from Kibbutz Nir Oz, whom Hamas kidnapped on October 7. Through a series of well-researched posts, they shared Dancyg's life story, his dedication to social justice, and his left-wing ideals, showing that being a Zionist and being a liberal are not mutually exclusive.

On International Women's Day, they featured Tamar Kedem Siman Tov, an artist and aspiring mayor, whom Hamas murdered, along with her family, in the October 7 attack.

Another post included the story of Eitan and Yair Horn, Argentinian-Israeli brothers currently held hostage in Gaza. They emphasize the brothers' love of simple pleasures and the void that their absence has left in their communities.

The two women carefully craft each post with hours of research, not only highlighting the victims of the war, but also recommending relevant books and films. They plan to expand into broader aspects of Jewish history and culture.

Although still a small account, Our Shared Jewish History has reached a wide audience, interacting with other accounts dedicated to memorializing victims or advocating for hostages. The founders have noticed that posts about younger individuals tend to garner more engagement, probably because Instagram's user base skews younger.

Gottlieb and Goodman have big dreams for their page. They hope it will become a valuable tool, helping Jewish people to engage confidently in conversations about Israel and Jewish diversity, and counter the "white colonizer" stereotype. They want to showcase the special and unique aspects of the Jewish community, while also acknowledging the persecution many have faced.

While they do not expect to transform global opinions about Israel single-handedly, they see their work as a way to educate and empower the Jewish community. They believe that although it is challenging to change minds, awakening their own community to its rich history and diversity is a worthy and achievable goal.

Israeli Comedian Announces That He Will Keep the Sabbath for the First Time

Vered Weiss
World Israel News

On March 17, 2024, Israeli comedian Guy Hochman announced on social media that he would observe Shabbat for the first time ever, and he invited his hundreds of thousands of social media followers to do the same.

Hochman said he is choosing to observe Parshat Zachor, the Shabbat immediately preceding Purim, in honor of the commandment to erase the memory of Amalek, the nation identified in the Bible as the arch-nemesis of the Jewish people.

Shortly after the October 7th atrocities, Israeli Prime Minister Benjamin Netanyahu spoke of the need to eliminate Hamas and invoked the commandment to erase the memory of Amalek.

Netanyahu said, "'Remember what Amalek did to you' (Deuteronomy 25:17). We remember and we fight."

Born in Ramat Gan, Hochman, the star of YouTube's "Nice Guy" channel, wrote on Instagram: "I might not be religious, but I am a very proud Jew, and we all remember and need to remember, October 7th."

He added "Next Shabbat, Shabbat Zachor, the Shabbat of 'Remember what Amalek did to you,' directly before Purim — I will keep Shabbat for the first time in my life."

"I am not keeping Shabbat for the Redemption, but for the unity of Israel, and for our heroic soldiers at the front," Hochman explained.

"The heart of most of Israel is in the right place today. We are ready in our hearts. I say that we should keep one Shabbat, stop the divisive discourse, and bring the spirit of a shared destiny from the front to our homes," he added.

Hochman has many entertainment credits, his most recent including the YouTube "Nice Guy" channel, and "Looking for Direction," which he created for Keshet broadcasting. Hochman was the first Israeli comedian to perform in Dubai, shortly after the signing of the Abraham Accords.

Hochman served in the Nahal Brigade's 932nd Battalion, and during the war, he made many visits to IDF units to entertain soldiers and raise morale. For this, the Zionist Council of Israel awarded him its Badge of Heroes.

Unity in Adversity: President Herzog's Call to Action

Moshe Kaplan, MD

IN A TIME of crisis, which tests the very fabric of society, clarity emerges with a powerful voice. President Isaac Herzog stepped forward to articulate a vision that cuts through the noise, declaring Israel's war against terror groups in the Gaza Strip as a decisive battle between good and evil. For Herzog, this conflict is not a morally ambiguous struggle, but a clear-cut fight to preserve the values that underpin free societies worldwide.

"Everyone talks about complexity, but this moment is not a complex moment. There is absolute good here and there is absolute evil here. There is light here and there is darkness here," Herzog asserts. His words resonate with an unyielding conviction, echoing the sentiments of a nation determined to protect its people and its principles.

Expressing gratitude for the United States's support, both in public forums and through military aid, Herzog emphasizes the global nature of this struggle. "We are not alone in this war. We are fighting the war as part of the family of nations — of all those who seek justice, peace, and freedom — against an enemy that has proven that humanity and humanism are its enemy."

Herzog's message is one of solidarity and shared purpose, highlighting the unification of Israeli society in the face of adversity. The nation has come together, bridging religious and political divides to stand as one. "There are few moments in the history of a nation where there is so much at stake," Herzog emphasizes, pointing to a unity forged in the fires of recent conflict.

The President's words reflect a deep, communal grief that has touched nearly every home in Israel. "The brutal attack by our enemies was directed at the Jewish people, but it did not distinguish among blood. There is hardly a home in Israel where the ripples of the painful tragedy we experienced have not reached," he says. This shared sorrow, Herzog believes, is a testament to the nation's solidarity: "The depth of our shared grief proves: We are all one Israeli nation."

Herzog's vision of Israel is one of resilience and unwavering resolve. "We have a wonderful nation," he proclaims, "a nation that knows it has no other choice, has no other land, and has no other country." His words serve as a rallying cry, inspiring Israelis to embrace their shared identity and to stand firm in the face of existential threats.

In these trying times, Herzog's message is a beacon of hope and determination. It underscores the essential truth that in the battle for justice, peace, and freedom, the light of unity and righteousness will ultimately prevail over the darkness of terror and hatred.

A Fissiparous People

Moshe Kaplan, MD

THE MASSACRE OF October 7 inspired a unity that the Jewish people has not experienced in a long time. It moved soldiers to take on more mitzvot, and Jews from around the world to send money and equipment needed for the war effort and to come on missions of support for the people of Israel.

Several prominent individuals and organizations are actively developing programs that will encourage more unity among Jews. This chapter notes some of them.

The Power of Unity: Lessons from the *Be A Mensch* Foundation

These words from Proverbs beautifully capture the concept of unity: "As water reflects a face back to a face, so one's heart is reflected back to him by another." This profound idea is at the heart of the Be A Mensch Foundation's philosophy (www.beamensch.com), which strives to actualize the essence of unity among Jews.

Yet, the question persists: Why do Jews often find themselves in conflict with one another? Several factors contribute to this discord, including a lack of dialogue, fear of interaction, cognitive dissonance, and stereotypes stemming from inadequate education. These issues impede true unity among the Jewish people.

A striking example of this disunity is the rift between secular Jews and chareidim in Israel. This divide, according to five former Chiefs of Staff of the Israel Defense Forces (Ehud Barak, Moshe Ya'alon, Gabi Ashkenazi, Benny Gantz, and Gadi Eisenkot), poses a greater threat to the country than a nuclear bomb from Iran. In a rare joint interview on Israeli Channel 12 in August 2022, General Eisenkot emphasized, "The thing that most endangers the State of Israel in my eyes is the lack of solidarity in Israeli society." The other generals echoed this sentiment, highlighting that internal cohesion and solidarity are crucial for Israel's survival.

This internal threat mirrors the ancient wisdom of our Sages, who attributed the destruction of the second Beis HaMikdash and the subsequent exile to *sinas chinam*, or baseless hatred among Jews. The Passover Seder's story of the Four Sons reinforces this lesson. The wicked son, who excludes himself from the Jewish narrative, reminds us that unity is about inclusion and shared identity. Despite different levels of observance — whether Orthodox, traditional, Reform, or completely removed from religious practice — Jews must embrace each other as family. Historical tragedies like the Holocaust have shown that our enemies do not discriminate based on how we identify. Jewish suffering and celebration are collective experiences.

When Jews maintain common ground despite disagreements, they grow stronger. In contrast, losing sight of our core commonalities has historically led to severe consequences, such as exile and the loss of sovereignty in the Land of Israel. Unity, therefore, is essential for overcoming external threats and preserving Jewish identity.

The State of Israel, though imperfect, is the Jews' only homeland. It represents an anchor and a vital asset that we must protect. Standing by Israel transcends politics; it is about understanding the historical role and destiny of the Jewish state in Jewish lives. In times of political debate and divisive election results, unity around the shared belief that Israel is the singular homeland is paramount. Democracy in Israel might be tested when the majority's decisions are challenging, but the unity of the Jewish people must remain steadfast.

So, how can Jews achieve this unity? The *Be A Mensch* Foundation offers a practical approach, fostering acceptance of diversity with tolerance and respect, through dialogue and communication. Its motto, "The religious and the secular refuse to be enemies," encourages direct encounters to dispel stereotypes. When secular Jews meet chareidim, animosities often dissolve. The foundation also utilizes media to bridge gaps.

Professor Aaron Ciechanover, a Nobel laureate, underscores the importance of internal solidarity, warning that strife and hatred among different groups pose a greater threat than external enemies. The foundation's efforts prove that good values, such as care, respect, and love for every Jew, can unite even the most disparate groups.

A powerful example of this unity in action occurred in 2011, when Yehuda S., a young student and future staff member of *Be A Mensch*, addressed a large protest. By framing social justice as a Jewish value, he turned a secular protest into a unifying cause. His message of mutual responsibility and solidarity transformed the crowd's hostility into a powerful assertion of Jewish unity.

The *Be A Mensch* Foundation continues to demonstrate that chareidi Jews care about their secular counterparts, exemplified by acts of kindness, such as distributing food and water during protests. This care helps to vanquish *sinas chinam*, bringing hope and harmony to the Jewish people.

Unity among Jews is not just an ideal but a necessity. By embracing shared values, fostering dialogue, and showing genuine care for one another, the Jewish people can overcome internal divisions and face external threats with strength and solidarity. As the *Be A Mensch* Foundation exemplifies, when Jews stand together, they can achieve great things and ensure a brighter future for all.

Acheinu Worldwide Achdut Program

Acheinu Worldwide Achdut Program:
One People. One Family. One Fate.
Creating Jewish Unity in 50 Countries and Counting....
https://acheinu.world/

This is a time to focus on the fact that we are one people. Since October 7th, we have seen an unprecedented expression of care and unity amongst our people. Just days before Hamas's invasion of Israel, our nation was fractured and divided, but that feels like a distant memory. Because today we have come together like brothers, once again, to defend our people.

This is the beautiful power of *Am Yisrael*. This is what makes us proud to be Jewish.

Now, we are faced with an opportunity. We can enjoy this unity as a fleeting experience, or we can capitalize on these moments of *achdut* and use them as an impetus to create positive change in our lives. This is the time for each of us to do our utmost to foster unity — within our families, our neighborhoods, and our people at large. We have a unique opportunity to repair old relationships and forge new ones, a chance to close the damaging gaps within the Jewish people. Our enemies took advantage of our disunity, so the way to win this war is to reunite once again.

New Exhibit at Hostage Square Aims to Inspire Unity and Healing

Israel National News, March 31, 2024

A NEW ART EXHIBITION of 32 mosaic creations is currently being featured at Tel Aviv's Hostage Square in solidarity with residents of the Gaza Border communities. Students at the Neveh Channah High School, part of the Ohr Torah Stone educational network, created the exhibition, inspired by the spirits of national unity and healing.

"We conceived this project in the first weeks of the war out of a feeling of deep sadness and pain, but also out of a realization that we needed to express solidarity with those from the Gaza border whose lives were completely turned upside down in an instant," explains Sharon Brand, director of Neveh Channah's "Etrog" beit midrash, who initiated the project. "The concept of people being drawn out of their homes amidst the chaos of war and loss of family and friends was something that we struggled to comprehend, and through this expression, we were hoping to reach out and create a sense of unity between us here in Gush Etzion and the people of the border region."

Brand emphasized that this spirit of national unity

inspired the artists from the outset. "As residents of Gush Etzion, a region from which we had been expelled from amidst war only to be blessed to return and rebuild, our hope was to share a sense of faith that they, too, will soon be able to come back home."

The project involved the work of over 150 students, resulting in 32 individual mosaics that reflect the symbols of the 32 affected Gaza border communities. "This is the result of four months of planning, thought, and careful implementation. The process required the students to gain a deep understanding of the history and culture of the communities because we wanted to ensure they were really identifying with their works and would be able to reflect the spirit of return and rebuild even in the face of such utter destruction and pain."

At the launch event at Hostage Square, the students met with Itzik Tayar Buchstav, whose nephew Yogev Buchstav was among whom Hamas kidnapped. The terror group claims that he was killed. "We are holding on to the hope that this isn't true, and we are working to give each other strength with the hope that he's still alive," he told the students. "We call on everyone to keep him in your hearts and prayers and pray for Yogev ben Esther."

Tagel Ben Menachem, a tenth grader at Neveh Chanah who contributed to the mosaic installation, described the process as deeply personal. "As someone whose father and siblings were called to the reserves, the reality is that our connection to the war is through those who are in battle and those who have fallen. In our community of Alon Shvut alone, we have been forced to bury four soldiers, so that sense of loss is constantly with us. But we weren't really able to feel that real bond with the residents of the Gaza border region until this project gave us the chance to become connected to the families who went through, and are continuing to go through, these horrific traumas."

Rabbi Dr. Kenneth Brander, President and Rosh Yeshiva of Ohr Torah Stone, was the featured speaker at the ceremony. "Our being here is to show that we have a responsibility where every moment of the day we need to continue to do our utmost to secure the release of the hostages and the rebuilding of the destroyed communities. These are our brothers and sisters, our parents and grandparents, and they remind us that every Jew must care for the welfare of the other. This project is a remarkable example for all of us, that we cannot allow this issue to be forgotten and that we cannot leave the hostages, or the residents of the northern and southern border areas, behind. Every one of us must take responsibility to bring each and every one of them home."

Neveh Channah's Head of School, Ruhama Gebel Redman, added, "It's incredibly heartwarming to see how our students and staff were able to transform such intense pain into something so creative and educational that reflects such powerful ideas of solidarity. Our sincerest hope and prayer is that our national unity will help to usher in days of peace for all the people of Israel."

Stronger Together — One Nation, One Heart

Moshe Kaplan, MD

IT IS INCUMBENT upon each of us to recognize the importance of mutual caring and support, if we are to work for the survival of the Jewish people. If you would like to assist in strengthening the Jewish people, you can contact any of these organizations. Keep in mind that these are only a small percentage of the many organizations striving to create unity. Find the one that speaks to you the most. The Jewish people will survive. You can choose to be part of the problem or part of the solution.

Appendices

APPENDIX A

About the Authors

Miriam Adelson, MD

Miriam Adelson, MD is an Israeli-American physician, philanthropist, and political donor. Born in Tel Aviv to parents who fled Poland before the Holocaust, she served in the IDF as a medical officer. After earning a BS in Microbiology and Genetics from the Hebrew University of Jerusalem, she earned an MD, graduating *magna cum laude* from Tel Aviv University Faculty of Medicine.

She served as the chief internist in the emergency room at Tel Aviv's Rokach (Hadassah) Hospital. In 1986, she moved to Rockefeller University, where she specialized in drug addiction in collaboration with Mary Jeanne Kreek. In 1993, she founded a substance abuse center and research clinic. She and her husband opened the Dr. Miriam and Sheldon G. Adelson Research Clinic in Las Vegas seven years later.

Dr. Adelson has stated that "the top issue of the Jewish community is the survival of the Jewish people." Rabbi Shmuley Boteach described her as "arguably the proudest Jew I have met." A strong supporter of Israel, she has said that her heart is in that country and that she got "stuck" in America after meeting her husband.

In response to the October 7th, 2023, Hamas-led attack on Israel, Dr. Adelson published an op-ed in *Forbes Israel*, entitled "Dead to Us." Referring to the wave of pro-Palestinian protests occurring across various western cities and countries, Adelson stated, "Those ghastly gatherings of radical Muslim and Black Lives Matter activists, ultra-progressives, and career agitators, were nothing short of street parties. These people are not our critics. They are our enemies, the ideological enablers in the West of those who would go to any length to eradicate us from the Middle East and, as such, they should be dead to us."

Yvette Alt Miller, PhD

Dr. Yvette Alt Miller holds a PhD in International Relations from the London School of Economics and has taught at Northwestern University and the London Business School. She has lectured around the world. Her most recent book, *Portraits of Valor: Heroic Jewish Women You Should Know*, describes the lives of 40 remarkable women who lived in different eras and lands, giving readers a sense of the vast diversity of Jewish history and experience.

Cochav Elkayam-Levy, PhD

Cochav Elkayam-Levy is the recipient of several exemplary awards, including the Toll Public Interest Center's Award for Outstanding Pro Bono Leadership, the Exemplary Pro Bono Service Award, and the Public Service Award of the University of Pennsylvania. She was recognized by the Philadelphia Bar Association and received its

Award for Outstanding Achievement in Human Rights; served as Penn Carey Law's Rule of Law and Human Rights Fellow; and was the recipient of the Leboy-Davies Award in Gender, Sexuality & Women's Studies from the Alice Paul Center for Research on Gender, Sexuality & Women.

Her research, which is published in top U.S. legal journals, centers on women's international human rights, national security issues, domestic implementation of international human rights law, religious liberties, transformative social changes, feminist theories, and sustainable development.

Before arriving at Penn, Dr. Elkayam-Levy served as a legal counsel for the Human Rights Division under the Deputy Attorney General of Israel (International Affairs). In that capacity, she consulted to the government on the implementation of human rights standards, and participated in international negotiations and international discussions. Dr. Elkayam-Levy also served as an associate with the Supreme Court Department of the Israeli Attorney General's Office.

After Hamas's murderous attack, and as the evidence about gender-based war crimes unfolded, Dr. Elkayam-Levy established The Civil Commission on Oct. 7th Crimes by Hamas against Women and Children, which is an independent, non-governmental collaboration of international human rights experts and women's rights organizations. The Commission advocates for and supports the investigation Hamas's war crimes against women and children during the massacre on October 7, 2023, and the continuous war crimes against abducted women and children. To this end, legal professional and academic researchers, and experts in international law, humanitarian and human rights law, victimology, and gender-based violence, together with representatives of Israeli women and human rights organizations, have come together with the purpose of gathering and distributing authentic information, providing expert advice, and advocating for and initiating actions related to the collection of evidence and testimonies on sexual and other crimes committed against women and children during the Hamas attack on October 7th. The commission collaborates with local and international entities, in full compliance with the international community's established international law and norms, including relevant UNSC resolutions on Women, Peace, and Security.

Brig. Gen. (ret.) Meir Elran, PhD

Brig. Gen. (ret.) Meir Elran is a senior researcher and director of the domestic research cluster of INSS, which includes research programs for Homeland Security and resilience, the Arab citizens in Israel, Society-Military and Israeli economics, and national security. Brig. Gen. (ret.) Elran served in the IDF as a career officer for 24 years, holding senior command and staff positions, primarily in the Military Intelligence Directorate. His last post was as deputy director of Military Intelligence.

Dr. Elran took an active role in the peace talks with Egypt and was an active member of the military delegation to the peace talks with the Hashemite Kingdom of Jordan. Following his retirement from the military, Dr. Elran served as the chief of staff of the Tel Aviv municipality and later, as a senior consultant for strategic planning for government offices, including the Ministries of Defense, Education, and Internal Security, and the National Security Council.

Dr. Elran's main areas of academic research are homeland security, disaster management, and societal resilience in face of protracted terrorism. Dr. Elran has published numerous papers on these subjects and edited several memoranda and volumes. He holds a BA from the Hebrew University in Jerusalem in Political Science and Middle East Studies, an MA from Indiana University in International Relations and Russian Studies, and a PhD in Political Science from the Haifa University. Dr. Elran also teaches at the University of Chicago in the Committee on International Relations.

Nils A. Haug

Nils A. Haug is an author and columnist. A trial lawyer by profession, he is member of the International Bar Association, the National Association of Scholars, and the Academy of Philosophy and Letters. Retired from law, his field of interest is political theory connected to current events. His work has appeared in *First Things Journal, The American Mind, Quadrant, Minding the Campus*, and the Gatestone Institute.

Rabbi Yair Hoffman

Rabbi Yair Hoffman has authored a number of books on Torah topics and often writes for VIN News, among others.

Meredith Jacobs

An award-winning journalist and author of several books, **Meredith Jacobs** is CEO of Jewish Women International

(JWI), a 125-year-old nonprofit dedicated to ending violence against women and girls. Jacobs has shepherded the development of numerous JWI initiatives, including the National Center on Domestic & Sexual Violence in the Jewish Community; the Collaborative of Jewish Domestic Violence Agencies; the Women's Financial Empowerment Institute; ReStart: job readiness for survivors; the Jewish Communal Women's Leadership Project; Men as Allies: Leading Equitable Workplaces; the Jewish Gun Violence Prevention Roundtable; and the international expansion of Young Women's Leadership Network. Under her leadership, JWI is spearheading state-wide advocacy efforts to achieve just lending practices, getting survivors of financial abuse access to bank loans that would set them on the path to long-term economic security.

Jacobs serves on the expert panel on Improving Access to Services for Domestic Abuse Victims in the Military, sponsored by the Department of Defense. She earned a BA in English from Haverford College and holds an MSc in Business from Johns Hopkins University.

The article that Jacobs contributed to this book was originally published in the *Forward* on November 27, 2023.

Moshe Kaplan, MD

A trained psychoimmunologist, **Moshe Kaplan, MD** served as Chief Medical Officer for the United States Coast Guard. While practicing medicine in San Francisco, he assisted Dr. Naomi Remen at Stanford Medical School in drafting a curriculum for an ideal healthcare system, which is still used in many medical schools today. In 1986, he moved to Israel. From 1987 to 2017, Kaplan served as Medical Director of an emergency medical services group in his local community in Jerusalem, including when the EMS group became the Har Nof representative of Magen David Adom in 1990.

He compiled *A Wholly Life* (Targum Press) and *Be A Mensch: Why Good Character Is the Key to a Life of Happiness, Health Wealth, and Love* (Gefen Press - English / Yedbooks - Hebrew). He currently is the CEO of the *Be A Mensch* Foundation (www.beamensch.com).

Karmit Klar-Chalamish, PhD

Karmit Klar-Chalamish is a lawyer and teacher, and she has written extensively on the use of restorative justice practices in cases of sexual abuse. She holds a PhD from Bar-Ilan University in Conflict Resolution, Management, and Negotiation (CRMN), and an MA from its College of Management Academic Studies, School of Behavioral Sciences (Family Studies). She teaches Law and Conflict Resolution, Management and Negotiation at Bar-Ilan University and teaches in the Department of Criminology as well. She is currently the head of the research department at The Association of Rape Crisis Centers in Israel, and has served in the past as the Director of Legal Advocacy Department at the HaSharon Rape Crisis Center. Dr. Klar-Chalamish was also on the Israeli team of the CSiS (Child Safeguarding in Sport) Project — a joint project of the European Union (EU) and Council of Europe (COE).

Douglas Murray

Douglas Murray is a bestselling author and journalist. His books include the *Sunday Times* number-one bestsellers *The War on the West: How to Prevail in the Age of*

Unreason; *The Strange Death of Europe: Immigration, Identity and Islam*; and *The Madness of Crowds: Gender, Race and Identity*. He has been Associate Editor and regular writer at the *Spectator* magazine since 2012, and contributes to other publications, including the *Wall Street Journal*, *The Times*, the *Sunday Times*, the *Sun*, the *Mail on Sunday* and the *New York Post*. A regular guest on broadcast news channels, he has also spoken at numerous universities, parliaments, the O2 Arena, and the White House.

Fiamma Nirenstein

Fiamma Nirenstein is an award-winning journalist and author, and former member of the Italian Parliament. The pivotal focus of Nirenstein's work is the fight against totalitarianism and terrorism, and its connection to antisemitism and the hate for Israel. Nirenstein is an expert on the Middle East conflict, terrorism, and antisemitism. Nirenstein works to give voice to Muslim dissidents. She served in the Council of Europe in Strasbourg, established and chaired the Committee for the Inquiry into Anti-Semitism, and is a founding member of the international Friends of Israel Initiative. In 2011, she established a center on Foreign Policy, "SUMMIT," to support dialogue between Europe and Middle East, focusing on human rights and democracy.

Her contribution in this book is an adaptation of her eyewitness account of what happened on October 7, 2023.

Ami H. Orkaby

Ami H. Orkaby was noted by *Forbes Magazine*, special Israeli edition, at the 42nd place out of the "300 list" of

Israel's most influential individuals. He is of counsel to the firm, Meitar Law Offices. Ami heads the firm's Immigration, Corporate Global Mobility and Relocation practice. Ami also holds vast expertise in crisis management and risk and compliance matters and representation of individuals, corporations before regulators and government bodies.

Ami acts as the sole legal adviser in Israel for the Governments of Japan, the Republic of South Korea and Mongolia, covering a wide range of matters on Israeli law and regulations.

Ami served as senior adviser at the Israeli Prime Minister's Office (2000-2004), Advising the highest levels of the Israeli government on issues ranging from legal to social and economic affairs.

In parallel, Ami represents high-net-worth individuals and corporations in a broad range of international and domestic corporate and commercial transactions, with emphasis on mergers and acquisitions, private equity financings, venture capital, technology transactions, banking and advisory work. Ami has substantial experience in structuring and negotiating complex cross border transactions primarily in the Asian region. Ami is the Chairman and Co-founder of MAC Fund, the First Israel-Korea Venture Capital Fund. In 2024, Ami Orkaby joined Trepont Fund as a partner. Trepont is a newly formed deep-tech fund bridging Korea, Israel, and Silicon Valley.

In 2006, Ami was appointed as the Honorary Consul General of Mongolia to Israel, and in 2010 he was appointed Honorary Consul General for the Republic of Korea in Jerusalem. Ami serves as Dean of the Israel Consular Corps. In 2010, Ami was elected President of the

Israel-Korea Chamber of Commerce. In 2003, Ami was one of few Israelis ever to receive the prestigious Eisenhower Fellowship for outstanding leadership.

Sheryl Sandberg

Sheryl Kara Sandberg is an American technology executive, philanthropist, and writer. Throughout her career, she has held highly influential positions within many global entities — from serving as a research assistant at the World Bank and Chief of Staff to the US Secretary of the Treasury, to vice president of global online sales and operations at Google, and COO of Facebook/Meta Platforms. She also serves on the boards of Women for Women International, the Center for Global Development, and V-Day.

Sandberg's book *Option B* (co-authored with Adam Grant) puts emphasis on grief and resilience when facing life's challenges. It offers practical tips for creating resilience in the family and community. She runs the Sheryl Sandberg & Dave Goldberg Family Foundation as an umbrella for her charitable endeavors and organizations promoting feminine leadership and global resilience.

Carol Ann Schwartz

Carol Ann Schwartz is Hadassah's 28th national president, and has been involved in Hadassah for more than 30 years, displaying her devotion to the organization, the Jewish community, and Israel. Before assuming the national presidency, she served as chair of Hadassah's National Speakers Bureau, and was a Hadassah representative to the American Zionist Movement and a member of the Hadassah Medical Organization's Board of Directors.

Before that, she served as national secretary and as one of six vice presidents. She has held many other national positions and chaired or served on national committees, following regional and local leadership positions.

Schwartz has an MBA from Cincinnati's Xavier University and has been an executive at The Morris Investment Company, which her grandfather founded. A highly regarded civic leader, Schwartz has served on the boards of the Jewish Federation of Cincinnati, Jewish National Fund-Cincinnati Region, Rockwern Academy, the University of Cincinnati Hillel, Adath Israel Congregation, the Israel Innovation Fund, and the Sigma Delta Tau Foundation. She has also served on the Jewish Agency for Israel's Israel and Overseas Committee.

Yaakov Shwekey

Yaakov Shwekey is a popular Orthodox Jewish recording artist and musical entertainer. He is of Egyptian and Syrian Sephardic heritage from his father's side, and Ashkenazi from his mother's side.

Wendy Singer

Wendy Singer served for nine years as executive director at Start-Up Nation Central (SNC). Today she is a strategic advisor to select Israeli startups and other organizations. Previously, she was steeped in the policy and Israel-advocacy world, including a decade on Capitol Hill, and 16 years as head of AIPAC's Israel office.

Noa Tohar Tishby

Noa Tohar Tishby is an Israeli activist, actress, model, producer, and writer. Tishby focuses on Zionist activism, and founded the advocacy organization Act for Israel in 2011. Tishby created the group to help correct misinformation about Israel's history, culture, and governmental policies. In 2014, she founded Reality Israel, which holds "leadership trips" to Israel for Jewish and non-Jewish people. In 2016 and 2018, she spoke before the United Nations General Assembly in New York City in support of Israel. In 2021, she published her first book, *Israel: A Simple Guide to the Most Misunderstood Country on Earth*.

In April 2022, then-Prime Minister Yair Lapid appointed Tishby as Special Envoy for Combating Antisemitism and the Delegitimization of Israel. She was the first person to serve in the newly created position, which she held for a year. Since the start of the 2023 Israel-Hamas war, Tishby has been a leading Zionist voice in the U.S.

Abraham J. Twerski, MD

Dr. Abraham Joshua Heshel Twerski (1930-2021) was an American Hassidic rabbi, a scion of the Chernobyl Hassidic dynasty, and a psychiatrist specializing in substance abuse.

In his rabbinic career Dr. Twerski was a prolific writer of Jewish books and Torah-themed lectures. He was co-spiritual leader of Congregation Beth Jehudah with his father until 1959.

Dr. Twerski's medical career included founding the Gateway Rehabilitation Center, for which he served as medical director emeritus. He was clinical director of the Department of Psychiatry at St. Francis Hospital in Pittsburgh, associate professor of psychiatry at the University of Pittsburgh's School of Medicine, and founder of the Shaar Hatikvah rehabilitation center for prisoners in Israel.

While Dr. Twerski's clinical career specialized in alcoholism and addiction, much of his popular writing concerned self-improvement and ethical behavior. He merged Jewish ethics and morality with the Twelve-Step Program and ideas from clinical psychology.

Dr. Twerski used to say, "One cannot consider oneself to be truly observant if one neglects Jewish ethics and morality." For him, this entailed dealing with "the psychological mechanism of *denial* [which] can blind a person to even the most obvious self-destructive behavior."

Gary Willig

Gary Willig is a veteran staff member of *Arutz Sheva's* news staff.

APPENDIX B

The *Be A Mensch* Foundation

The *Be A Mensch* Foundation is an organization in Israel (www.beamensch.com) that promotes unity between religious and secular Jews through dialogue groups that emphasize tolerance, respect, and consideration based on conflict resolution and the book *Be A Mensch: Why Good Character is the Key to a Life of Health, Happiness, Wealth, and Love* (Gefen Press - English / Yedbooks - Hebrew).

The organization has approbations from Nobel Laureates, from Tal Brody, Rachael Fraenkel, Nathan Sharansky, and other notables.

We Prepared for Oct. 8th Ten Years Ago

In Israel, tragedies unite us — but for how long? On Oct. 6th, the population in Eretz Yisrael was fractured. On Oct. 8th, the country reunited in tears and outrage. Historically, unity galvanized by grief can be short-lived. Unity founded on common identity, values, and purpose persists.

Who are we to say that?

We are the *Be A Mensch* Foundation. For over a decade,

we've been the go-to address for bridging the *Chareidi–Chiloni* divide in Israel. Popular shows such as *Srugim* and *Shteisel* inspired the secular public to want to meet and understand the Torah community living on its periphery.

Be A Mensch facilitates communication, connections, and a comfortable setting in which to explore uncomfortable issues. After a decade of effort, the results have been stellar, as the Ministry of Education, the Israeli Scouts, the IDF, and now C-level business executives have turned to us to create *achdut* (unity) between the disparate communities. Consider these points of focus:

- IDF: *Be A Mensch* meets regularly with IAF fighter pilots and flight crews to help them discover their cultural and spiritual roots in Jewish history and heritage. Many express a zealous desire to learn Torah sources once they understand the basis for unity.
- *Be A Mensch* has hosted unity encounters with over 8,600 high school students in 37 liberal Israeli schools. Principals, teachers, parents, and students declare this is a "must have" experience. (*BAM* has a tender from the Ministry of Education to meet with student groups up to four times per year. This program reaches 50,000 students.)
- Israel Scouts (*HaTzofim*) become future leaders in Israeli society. *Be A Mensch* conducts weekly meetings, spanning several years, to create deep, meaningful relationships. These often lead participants to take on lasting commitments to Jewish living and learning.
- Israeli C-level high-tech executives have reached out to *Be A Mensch* to learn Torah sources for business

practices, as well as how to establish homes founded on genuine Jewish values and practices.
- During the angry protests last year, *Be A Mensch* disarmed hatred and generated calm, understanding, and sanity during two demonstrations in Bnei Brak.
- Our latest frontier has just opened, as we apply our social healing algorithm in the Israeli university system. We recently launched a one-year, for-credit program with the Hebrew University in Jerusalem.

The imperative behind *Be A Mensch* is a concept everyone agrees is essential to a healthy, functional society. We invite you to explore what's working in Israel and discover how the *Be A Mensch* principles can work in your community, as well.

To date, we've engaged over 35,000 secular Israelis.

Our access: Over 500,000 future leaders and influencers in Israel.

www.beamensch.com/video

APPENDIX C

Sources

AFP and TOI staff. (April 1, 2024), October 7 survivor stars on Israel's amputee soccer team *(excerpts). The Times of Israel.*

Asa-El, *Amotz.* (Dec. 1, 2023). The anti-Zionist sex: Feminist organizations side with Hamas (excerpts). *The Jerusalem Post.*

Attali, Amichai. (Aug. 7, 2024). The Israeli spirit is unmatched anywhere (excerpts).*YNet News.*

Avitan Cohen, Shirit (May 7, 2024). They unloaded bodies from the car, like in the Holocaust (excerpts). *Israel Hayom.*

Botbol, Amelie. (May 14, 2024). A Story of Unity and Hope: Surviving Hamas Captivity (excerpts). *Jewish New Syndicate,*

Botbol, Amelie. (May 29, 2024). The Heroic Escape of Yarin Shriki: A Tale of Survival and Strength (excerpts). *Jewish News Syndicate.*

Cohen, Ben. (March 8, 2024). October 7: Rape as an instrument of genocide. (excerpts). *The Jewish News Syndicate.*

Grenny, Joseph. How to Confront a Liar (excerpts). *Crucial Learning*

Hoffman, Yair. (Feb. 21, 2025). Charles Manson and the Bibas Victims of Hamas. *VIN New.com.*

Jacobson, Zachary Jonathan. (May 21, 2018). Many are worried about the return of the "Big Lie." They're worried about the wrong thing *(excerpts). The Washington Post.*

Kaplan, Seymour, Harvard Law School '39. Personal communication from. The Role of Ivy League Universities.

Kashti, Or. (April 12, 2024) "I Won't Work with You. You're Committing Genocide": Israeli Academia Faces an Unprecedented Global Boycott (excerpts). *Haaretz.*

O'Donoghue, Rachel. (Aug. 19, 2024). Unmasked: The Pro-Hamas Sources Used by International Media (excerpts). *Honest Reporting*

Orkaby, Ami H. (Jan. 24, 2025). No peace with terror: International community must support a Hamas-free future. *The Jerusalem Post.*

Pachter, Sarah. (Nov. 3, 2024). This man rescued 120 people on Oct. 7th. Aish.com.

Perlberger, Hanna. (April 17, 2024). Anti-Fragility: The Jewish People's Resilience During Dark Times (excerpts). *Aish.com.* (excerpts)

Rosenberg, Yair. (Sept. 22, 2022). How Anti-Semitism Shaped the Ivy League as We Know It *(excerpts). The Atlantic.*

Ruda, Bennett. (April 1, 2024). Hamas's strategy is to create a false perception of reality. (excerpts) *Jewish National Syndicate*

Startup Nation Central. (Sept. 12, 2024). Israel's tech sector shows resilience, but future growth depends on regional stability and responsible government.

Sudilovsky, Judith. (April 15, 2024). The Bedouin lawyer helping Israel back on its feet. *Israel 21c*

The Hartman Institute event. (May 8, 2024) Remarkable resilience: Leading the way forward.

Times of Israel Staff. (July 24, 2024). Male October 7 Survivor Recounts Rape at Hands of Hamas Terrorists.

TOI staff. (May 23, 2024). IDF airs interrogation clips of terrorist father and son confessing to rape on Oct. 7 (excerpts). *The Times of Israel.*

U.S. Embassy. (Feb. 2, 2024). President Herzog broadcasts live from the Western Wall to the March for Israel in Washington, D.C.

Willig, Gary. (Feb. 25, 2025). The most evil society in human history. *Israel National News.*

Willig, Gary. (Oct. 8, 2023). The new 9/11. *Israel National News.*

Woodhams, J., Taylor, P. J., Cooke, C. (Jan. 1, 2020). Multiple perpetrator rape: Is perpetrator violence the result of victim resistance, deindividuation, or leader-follower dynamics?" (excerpts). *Psychology of Violence.*

Zanger-Nadis, Maya. (April 4, 2024). Post-Oct. 7 antisemitism spurs pair to use hostages' roots to highlight Jewish diversity. *The Times of Israel.*